Toni Onley's

British Columbia

A Tribute

RAINCOAST BOOKS

Vancouver

For my daughter, Lynn, and my son, James, and for my fellow artist and pilot Robert Murray, who shares my passion for flying and painting

First published in 1999 by

Raincoast Books
8680 Cambie Street
Vancouver, B.C.
V6P 6M9
(604) 323 7100

1 2 3 4 5 6 7 8 9 10

CANADIAN CATALOGUING IN PUBLICATION DATA

Onley, Toni, 1928-
Toni Onley's British Columbia

ISBN 1-55192-256-8

1. Onley, Toni, 1928- 2. Watercolour painting. 3. British Columbia – In art. I. Title.
ND249.O58A4 1999 759.11 C99-910342-3

The Canada Council for the Arts since 1957 | Le Conseil des Arts du Canada depuis 1957

Raincoast Books gratefully acknowledges the support of the Government of Canada, through the Book Publishing Industry Development Program, the Canada Council and the Department of Canadian Heritage. We also acknowledge the assistance of the Province of British Columbia, through the British Columbia Arts Council.

Designed by Leslie Smith
Map by Eric Leinberger

Printed and bound in Canada

CONTENTS

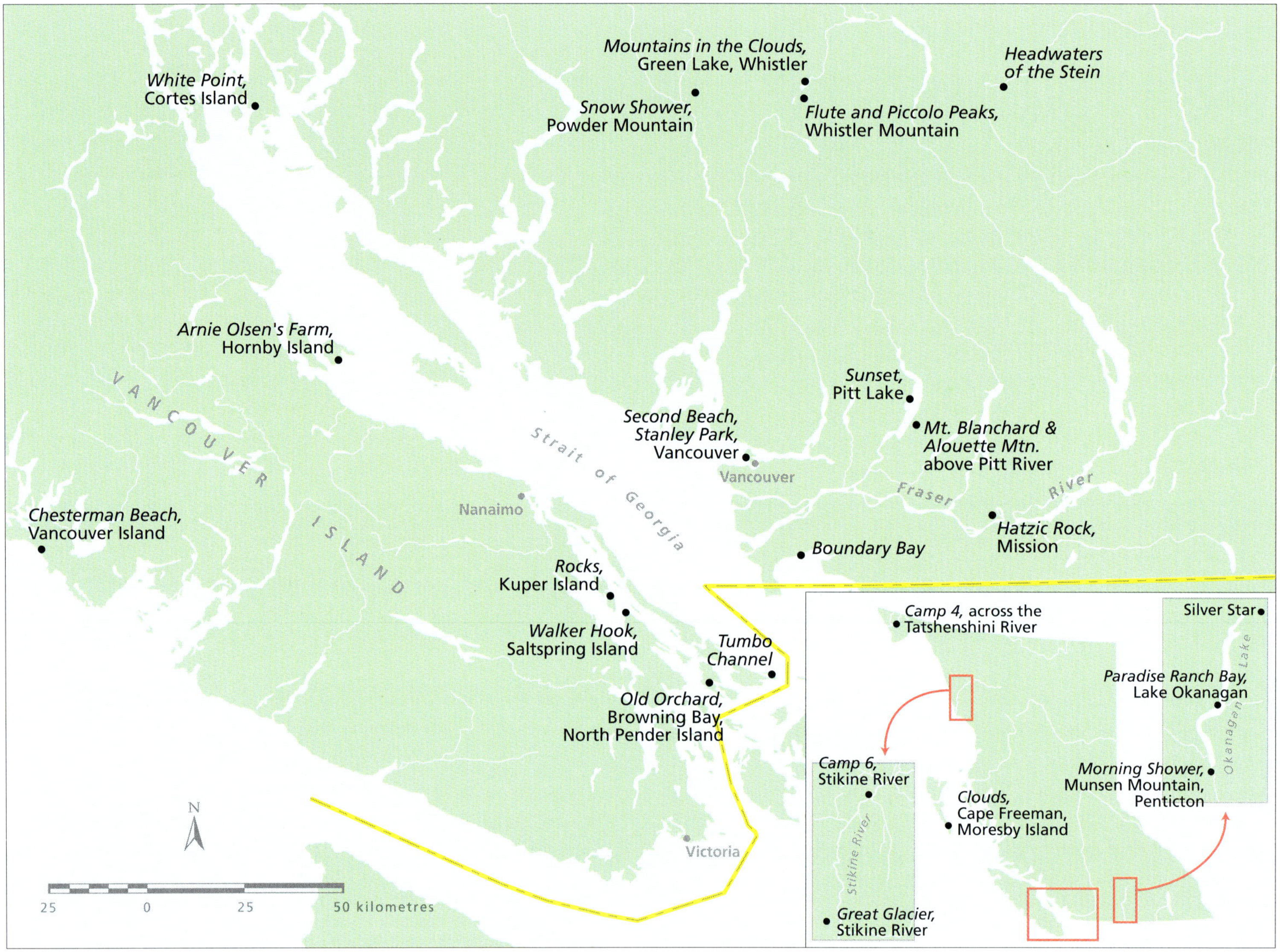
White Point,
Cortes Island
Mountains in the Clouds,
Green Lake, Whistler
Headwaters
of the Stein
Snow Shower,
Powder Mountain
Flute and Piccolo Peaks,
Whistler Mountain
Arnie Olsen's Farm,
Hornby Island
Sunset,
Pitt Lake
VANCOUVER
Second Beach,
Stanley Park,
Vancouver
Mt. Blanchard &
Alouette Mtn.
above Pitt River
Strait of Georgia
Vancouver
Fraser
River
Nanaimo
Chesterman Beach,
Vancouver Island
ISLAND
Hatzic Rock,
Mission
Boundary Bay
Rocks,
Kuper Island
Walker Hook,
Saltspring Island
Tumbo
Channel
Old Orchard,
Browning Bay,
North Pender Island
Camp 4, across the
Tatshenshini River
Silver Star
Okanagan Lake
Paradise Ranch Bay,
Lake Okanagan
Camp 6,
Stikine River
Morning Shower,
Munsen Mountain,
Penticton
Clouds,
Cape Freeman,
Moresby Island
Stikine River
Great Glacier,
Stikine River
N
Victoria
25
0
25
50 kilometres

PREFACE

My earliest memory of painting in watercolour is from grade one at the Catholic school I attended on the Isle of Man where I was born in 1928. The beginning years were taught by nuns. Once my teacher had set us the task of painting a daffodil. I thought I had done very well because even then I knew I was an artist, but my teacher pointed out with her cane that a daffodil had six petals, not seven as I had painted. She then beat me with her cane to drive home the lesson. After that I thought of her as Our Lady of Perpetual Suffering. The memory of her litany of punishments and the seven-petalled daffodil will stay with me forever.

The minutes of school I spent chained to a desk passed like hours, just waiting for the long summer holidays which I would always spend with my paternal grandparents in the little town of Ramsey in the north of the island.

My grandmother, who was an Irish lady from Queenstown (now Cork), county Cork, always claimed my talent for painting came from her, because as a girl she had designed Irish lace. I remember, when I was ten years old, going on long walks with her on summer afternoons through glens and mountains, along coastal trails, she with her book of verse and me with my little box of watercolours. We would rest on the brow of a hill, I would paint and she would read to me Wordsworth or Keats.

I was about fourteen before I received any formal art training. I enrolled in the Douglas School of Art in my hometown, where I was taught perspective, illuminated addressing, uncial script and the studious copying of the Book of Kells. We were taught life drawing and etching, but apart from illuminated addressing, which has influenced my handwriting ever since, I cannot remember learning anything of lasting value. However, it was at this time that I fell under the influence of John Hobbs Nicholson, the lettering teacher.

Nicholson was a fine watercolour painter of the school of nineteenth century English masters like Cotman and de Wint, and I was spellbound by his technique. When I found out that he took a group of favoured senior students outdoor painting every weekend, I begged to be allowed to join and was reluctantly allowed as I was the youngest. We painted in foul weather and fine. Often, when all the other students had dropped out in mid-winter, John Hobbs and I would cycle out manfully into the ice and wet snow alone, adding glycerin to our watercolours to prevent them from freezing.

Nicholson was an unbending master of the medium of watercolour. He poured scorn on abstract art and all fashionable art of the day, freeing me from such concerns to study what was before me – light and cloud shadows racing across a landscape. "Look and paint and don't look back," he would say, and I did, feeling at one with Nature and the nature of watercolour, even though a war was raging in Europe and the night sky filled with silent flashes from bombs dropped on the far-off mainland. I felt remote from war, concerning myself only with the joy of painting in watercolour and exploring my island in search of subjects.

The Isle of Man's only export is its people. In 1948, it was time for me and my family to leave for the new world. My father, who was an actor, started a theatrical touring company called, naturally enough, The New World Theatre Company, and for two years he and a small cast of actors brought Shakespeare via school bus to every one-silo town in Canada. I settled in Brantford, Ontario, and for the first time in my life was away from the sea. I wondered how I could paint this new, sharp-focused land.

I looked at Canadian painting for a clue, knowing of course I would have to find my own way. The Group of Seven offered no answers for me; nothing in my background could prepare me to paint in such an opaque way. But Tom Thomson could paint light and David Milne could handle watercolour in a way with which I could identify.

In 1951, Carl Schaefer came to teach a summer school at the Doon School of Art at Doon in Ontario. This was my first opportunity to meet an artist who had succeeded in recreating the crisp, strong line and colour of the rural Ontario with which I was now familiar. Carl was a good influence on me at that time as well as being a great deal of fun. He was forever dressing up in a Confederate army uniform and charging up and down the rolling hills. When he was finally out of sight, we could hear the distant report of his muzzle-loading musket. I admired his watercolours greatly, as I still do today. He gave me a start in seeing what was for me a new land.

The early 1950s were difficult economic times for me. There was little time for the pleasure of painting, only long hours of work that dies with the worker. This was before the Canada Council and before commercial galleries. Before the wheel. No one but Vincent Massey bought art. Even David Milne was slowly dying from his poor sales. In one year, 1952, I painted only one watercolour.

In the spring of 1955, I moved to British Columbia. My wife Mary had died and I was left with two daughters: Lynn, age two, and Jennifer, age four. My father's theatre company had run out of money and steam in Penticton in the beautiful Okanagan Valley. My parents invited me to come out west and start again. I firmly believe in running away, because it was after my arrival in Penticton that I once more had time to paint. I taught children's art classes and senior citizens' art classes and in between I painted the Okanagan hills and lakes.

The two years I spent in the Okanagan Valley gave me time to reflect on my past and what I was going to do with my future. From early childhood I had always thought of myself as an artist. Out of fear that I would cut off my ear and live off the family, my father had wisely articled me to a local architect when we lived on the Isle of Man. I worked for a time as an architectural draftsman in Penticton, but at twenty-nine, in 1957, the time had come for me to decide whether my future was to be in art or in architecture.

The decision was made for me. Like a message from heaven, I received a letter from Mexico to say I had won a scholarship from the Instituto Allende in San Miguel de Allende. It was all the excuse I needed. Even though I did not have enough money at the time to accept it, I would find a way. I had accumulated about 250 watercolours over the years. I hired an auctioneer and the Knights of Pythias Hall and sold them all for an average of $5.00 each, netting $1,250. I was on my way. I packed my art supplies and my two daughters into my little MG–TD sports car and headed for Mexico.

I had as much difficulty coming to terms with the Mexican landscape as I had when I arrived in Ontario nearly ten years earlier. I saw Mexico as black and white with occasional screaming primary colours. Mexico is a visually violent country to me. The mountains are unfriendly: they pierce the sky chaotically, then plunge into dark canyons. I responded to this landscape like a chameleon and did some of my most uncharacteristic watercolours. Many of these works were later torn up and destroyed, to become the material for my first collages.

These collages were to be my preoccupation for the next four years, taking me out of the landscape and into the studio. It was not until I spent a year in London from 1963-64 that I again started looking at watercolours.

In London, I visited the Prints and Drawings Room at the British Museum one day every week and rediscovered my roots. Here were the great nineteenth-century watercolour painters of England I had so fervently tried to emulate as a boy. I was meeting them again like old friends from a golden age. Little watercolours filled with light, space and spirit. I held them in my hands: William Turner's explosions of light; John Sell Cotman's solidly built compositions, building wash upon wash; and the loaded brushstrokes of David Cox. All my patron saints. I had come home to my source.

When I returned to Vancouver in 1964, I would climb down the ladder from my big works and reinvolve myself directly with landscape. The new landscapes would be different, informed by the compositional involvements of my minimalist collages of the past three years. They were now abstract paintings that had become landscapes in the doing. They were images that were archetypal as well as particular, personal as well as universal. These images would, over time, become less abstract and more directly paintings of particular landscapes.

From that time to the present, I have travelled widely. In addition to Canada and the U.S., I have painted in the Canadian Arctic, Italy and other European countries, Japan, China, New Zealand, India, Malaysia, Thailand, the Yukon and Alaska and, lately, in England, Ireland, Egypt and Bahrain in the Arabian Gulf. But after travelling the crowded earth, I always come home to British Columbia, to appreciate, time and time again, our great natural resources of space and endlessly varied topography.

Although I have often ventured into warmer regions, basically I am a northern temperament, most at home drying my watercolours in the clear, thin air of Arctic deserts, on British Columbia's glacial lakes and coastal islands, in Georgian Bay or in Japan, whose spiritual paths I cross and whose brushes I use.

Since 1975, I have used a Lake Amphibian, a modern flying boat, as my equivalent of Tom Thomson's canoe. It takes me to the most remote locations in British Columbia, where I may land on beaches or lakes, even the larger mountain lakes. For a short time in the early 1980s, I also owned a Polish-built ski-plane which allowed me to land on glaciers. With these two planes, for three years I was intimately acquainted with the mountains of the Whistler region. But now, having lost the ski-plane, as recounted later in this book, I must paint some mountains from a greater distance.

For the rich variety of landscapes to be explored in British Columbia, the medium of watercolour painting presents the perfect vehicle. From the mid-eighteenth to the end of the nineteenth-century in Britain, the medium became intimately bound up with the evolution of humanity's response to the natural world. It also remains the most portable of media. I can travel for weeks at a time with a small case containing my palette and fifty sheets of paper.

The earliest watercolour paintings in North America date from explorations of the New World when artists travelled with explorers like Captains Cook and Vancouver or crossed the mountains with Fraser.

George Back, a midshipman with Franklin from 1819 to 1822, recorded the tragic journey from Great Slave Lake to Bathurst Inlet in wonderful watercolour sketches and prose that capture the drama of Franklin's first Arctic overland expedition. These early watercolourists were topographers, recorders of fact, their works a far cry from Turner's pure washes of colour and light.

Topographical artists were not concerned, as I am today, to express a Zen-like oneness of humanity with Nature. They did not indulge themselves, as later British artists were to do and as I do today, in the romance of the landscape – in my case, a British Columbia landscape I share with poets and ecologists.

British Columbia is a land with soul. There is no other place in North America where you will find among its inhabitants such an instinct to protect Nature and such a determination to set an example of conservation for other countries. We are the custodians of one of the oldest living things on the planet, the giant Sitka spruce. It is here that the roots of the strongest ecology movement in the world began. It is no accident that International Greenpeace got its start here.

Flying out into the landscape in my amphibious flying boat, I go where there is no windsock or traffic controller to tell me in which direction the wind blows. Because I need to land into the wind, I look for telltale signs, like patterns on the water, a breaking wave or the reflections in sheltered water protected by a headland. A seagull perched on a rock will face into the wind. Leaves will shimmer on the windward side of a tree. A boat on a buoy will weather-cock into the wind. These are all signals that save the day for a pilot and make him safe, but also, like cloud observations, help me as a painter to notice the continuous changes that are taking place.

The finer characteristics of a scene, its loose freshness, can only be achieved by painting outdoors. So many artists make studies, take them home to use later, only to get it half right. Out of doors, one is forced to work quickly and surely and to take risks. An agility is called for which can be lost in the studio. Outdoors, I am faced with the fleeting effects of light and atmosphere, to be captured quickly or not at all.

That great master of watercolour, John Singer Sargent, praised his friend Hercules Brabazon for paintings in which he saw "immediate sensations flower again with a swiftness that makes one, for a time, forget there was a medium." Sargent described his own watercolours as "snapshots," a term borrowed from photography that expressed his ability to capture fleeting effects of light and shadow.

Racing cloud shadows across the landscape may turn a pale green headland into an ominous black whale of a shape. I have one eye on my paper in the excitement of getting it down, freezing the moment, the other on my flying boat, making sure it is well secured or that I am not stranded by a receding tide.

In the silence of the mountains, I can hear myself think or, better still, not think. In silence, space is cleared and time stayed. I need silence to respond fully to the subject at hand, silence to unclutter my mind. "All profound things and emotions of things are preceded and attended by Silence," wrote Herman Melville, whose greatest novel, *Moby Dick*, can now be read as a parable of the ecology movement.

Silence is the untouched white paper which gives meaning to those parts touched by the brush. During my effort some years ago at Shodo (calligraphy), I could never approximate my teacher's skill, until it dawned on me that what was called for was the accurate shaping of the negative forms, those parts of the paper untouched by the brush. The silence.

The simple linear and verbal way of understanding does not operate in true wilderness.Here we need to rely on the primitive unconscious. It wells up of its own accord, as we are overwhelmed and our inner balance is restored. The good paintings fall off the brush, the less successful take longer.

Leaving behind the armchair adventurers in cyberspace and the postmodern deconstructionists, I fly off to my lonely mountain lakes where, like a straw on the wind, I enter the real world of risk.

As Paul Zweig wrote in *The Adventurer*, "Man risking his life in perilous encounters constitutes the original definition of what's worth talking about." I have had my share of airplane crashes, but comfort myself with the knowledge that most accidents happen in the home. John Glenn came back from outer space only to slip in the bathtub. Yet still, he survived, to return to space once more.

TONI ONLEY,
Vancouver, January 1999

THE WATERCOLOURS

ARNIE OLSEN'S FARM

HORNBY ISLAND

Hornby Island is a year-round home or summer retreat for many B.C. artists and writers, including Tom Burrows, Gordon Payne, Vaughn Neville, Wayne Ngan, Jerry Pethick and the late Jack Shadbolt and his wife, Doris. I have many friends there whom I visit from time to time on my frequent painting expeditions to the Gulf Islands.

Hornby and nearby Savary Island exist within a microclimate which gives them less rain and more sunshine than the surrounding region. I can often find good weather there for painting or a safe haven for my plane when storms sweep across Vancouver Island and cut off visibility down Georgia Strait. My friend Arnie's summer place on Hornby is strategically placed for me at such times.

If Arnie is home, he will chase the cows off his field so I can land. There is really no such thing as bad weather, now that I think of it. It may not be great to fly in, but it's great to paint, looking out from a shelter into the storm.

An impromptu stop at Arnie's farm can offer all sorts of surprises. His guests, usually from the creative community, can make a layover into a wonderful evening. On a recent visit, John Bishop, Vancouver's preeminent restaurateur, produced an unforgettable dinner, starting with a crab bisque I can still taste in memory.

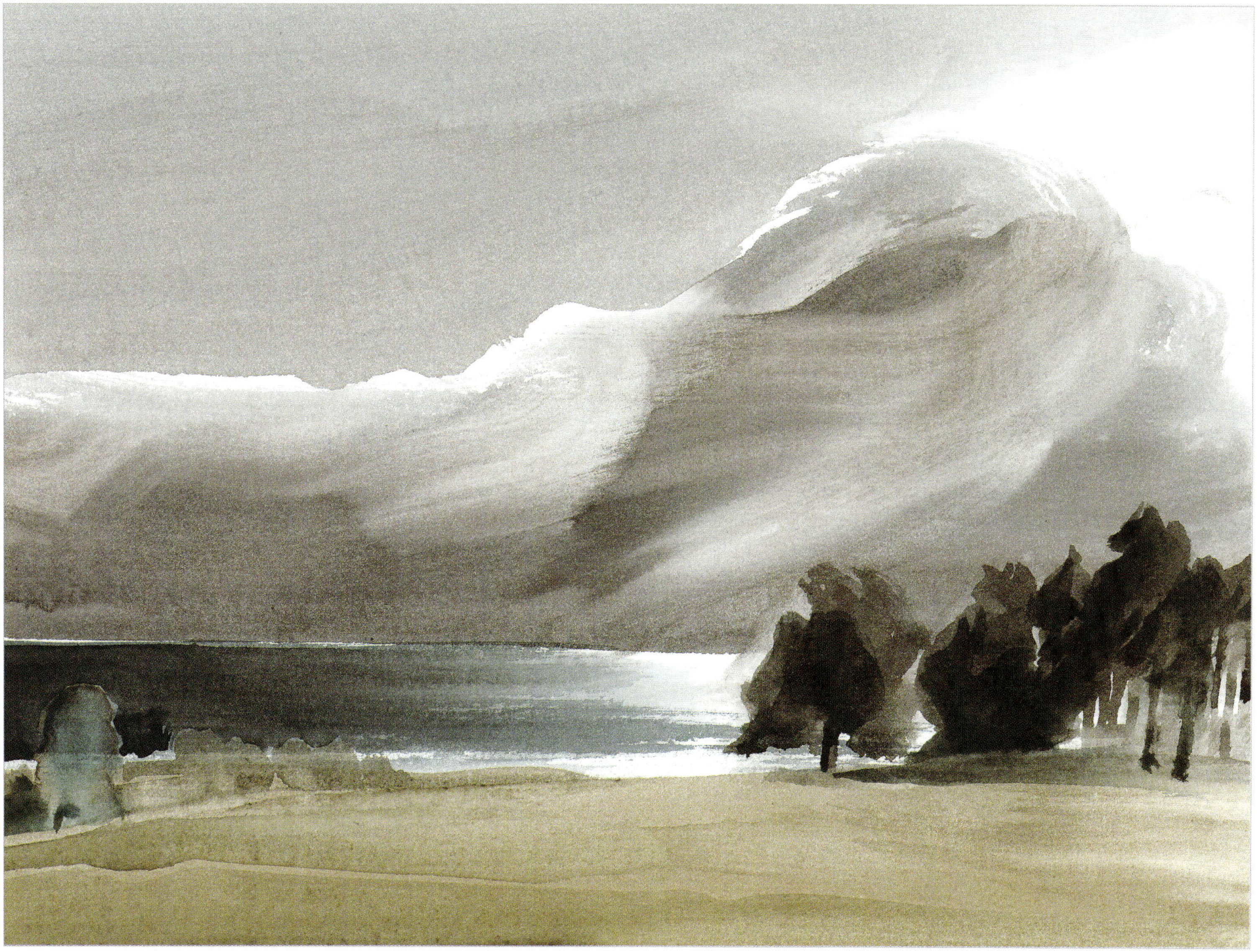

Arnie Olsen's Farm, Hornby Island, 23 August 1997

GREEN LAKE
WHISTLER

One of the great pleasures of watercolour is meditating on the compositional and atmospheric possibilities of its luminous transparencies. Painting is discovery, arriving at a point at which I surprise myself, creating a painting I could not have possibly imagined at the beginning.

When one is learning to paint in watercolour, the techniques of handling what can be a difficult medium are all important, and this is as it should be. Our art schools expect originality and personal insight far too soon, before the student has mastered the medium. I was fortunate to have been born on a remote island and to have known little of contemporary art until I was twenty. As a result, I was able to see my landscape eventually through my own eyes.

In this painting I was aiming at the apocalyptic side of English Romanticism, giving it full play, like Turner and his contemporary, the "mad" John Martin, who was considered by his contemporaries to be, along with Turner, among the greatest geniuses of all time.

Martin's strong individuality is what I most identify with. Extremities of self-expression ran in his family. His brother Jonathan, in a fit of rage against the Church of England, attempted to burn down York Minster, and his brother William was so eccentric that he barely escaped the asylum. But there is no compelling evidence to show that John Martin was anything but sane. If anything, his madness was the passion of genius, which many find incomprehensible.

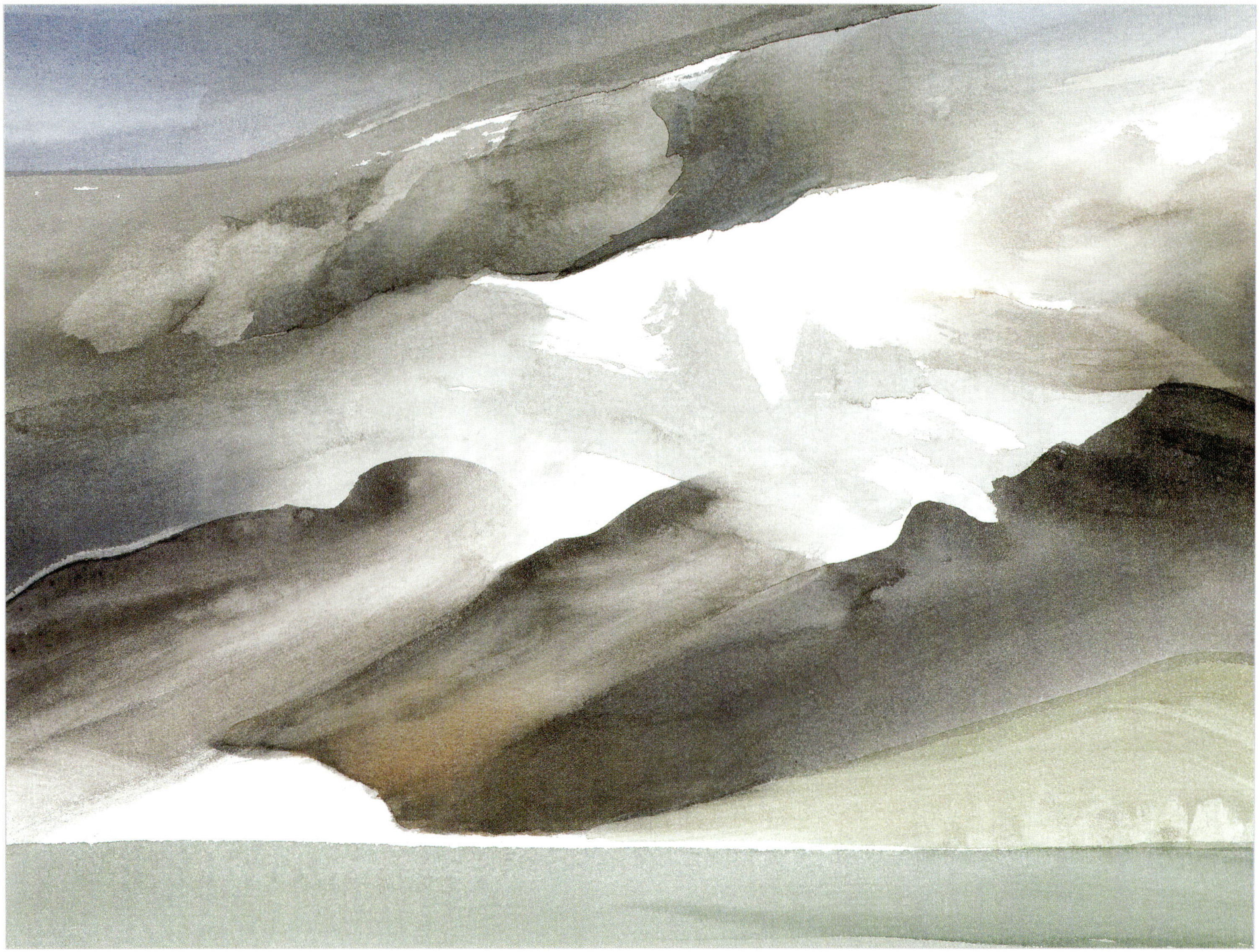

Mountains in the Clouds, Green Lake, Whistler, 17 August 1996

WHITE POINT

CORTES ISLAND

This Gulf Island is located fifteen miles east of Campbell River, Vancouver Island. A one hour flight for me in my flying boat, it is nine hours by car and ferry from Vancouver. For this reason, it is less inhabited than the Gulf Islands closer to Vancouver and has better retained its rugged mystery. Being close to the mainland Coast Range, it has wonderful views towards Desolation Sound.

Cortes Island was named in 1792 by the Spanish naval officers Galiano and Valdez, presumably after Hernando Cortez, the conqueror of Mexico. Regarding this general vicinity, Captain Vancouver wrote in his journal, "[it] affords not a single prospect that is pleasing to the eye." No connoisseur of landscape, he regarded the area as uninhabitable and, hence, "desolate."

This view of Cortes was painted the summer I taught at Hollyhock, a New Age school on the island. When I arrived, I ran my flying boat out of the water up onto a nearby sandy beach. I planned to leave it on the beach during the week I was teaching but soon discovered that the rising tide would drive it onto the drift logs, so I had to taxi around to Cortez Bay and tie it to a boat buoy where it could safely weathercock into the breeze.

Mystical subjects presented that year at Hollyhock included Hand Holding, Drum Beating, Anal Breathing, The Art of Sexual Ecstasy and Landscape Painting in Watercolour.

My stay was most enjoyable.

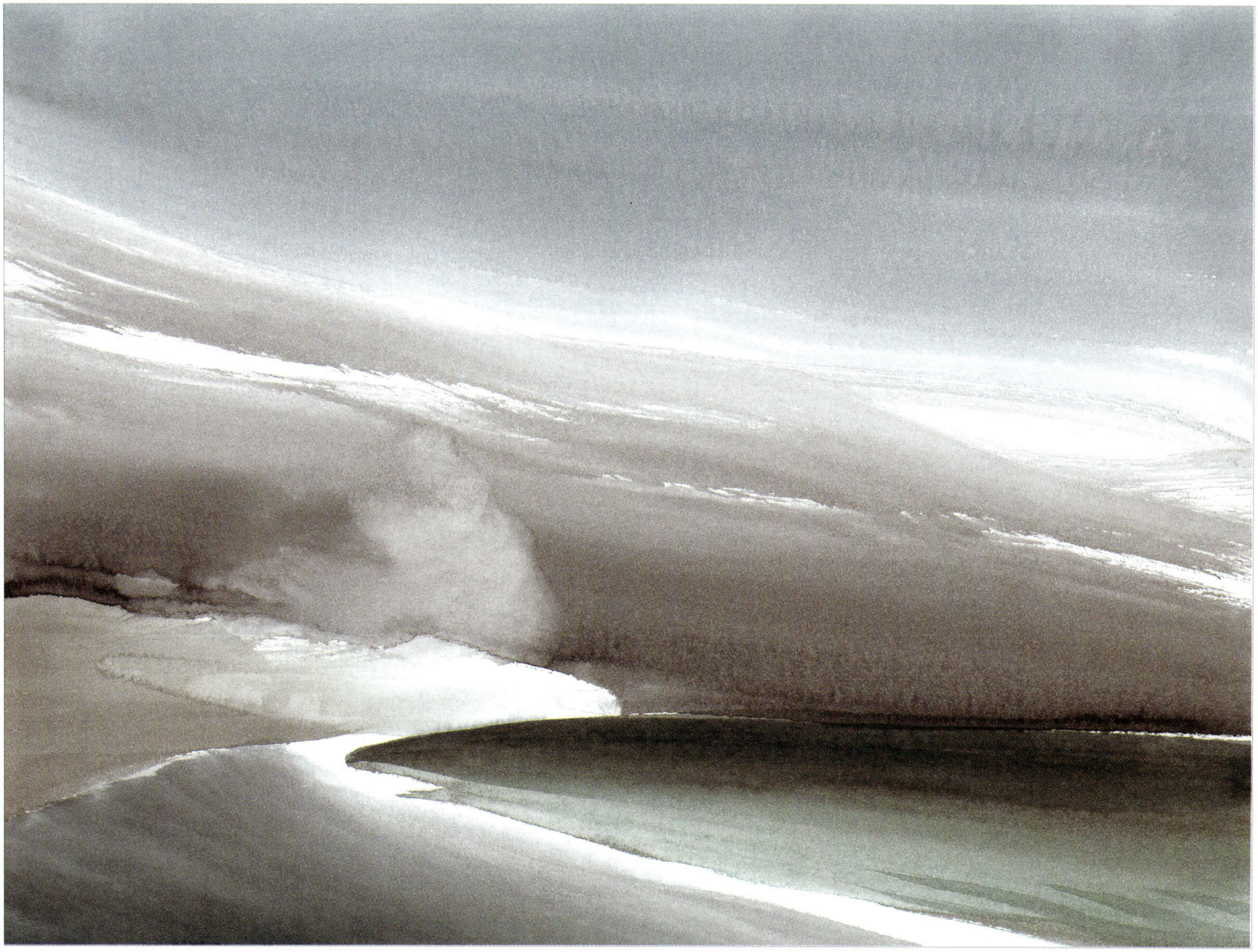

White Point, Cortes Island, 16 June 1994

CHESTERMAN BEACH

VANCOUVER ISLAND

One of the most dramatic stretches of coast in the world lies along the west coast of Vancouver Island. Each year I explore this coast, landing my airplane on the hard, surf-pounded beaches, camping for days on end.

According to my logbook, I first landed on the wave-hardened sands of Chesterman Beach in my first airplane, a tail-dragger called a Champion Sky-Trac, on 26 July 1969. That day I was exploring the beaches along the west coast of Vancouver Island from Long Beach to the pink sands of Flores Island to Nootka Sound. I used to find glass net floats that had drifted all the way from Japan, but not any more, for they are now made of plastic.

I set up my tent on Vargas Island's beautiful Ahous Bay, as I have done almost every year since. I still sleep under the stars there, watching the satellites moving steadily across the night sky as I listen to L.A. on the radio.

It is through the grandeur of Nature that the poet and the painter are drawn to self-understanding. Works done in these places are, in Wordsworth's expression, "spots in time" that anchor me forever to the places I return to year after year in the hope that nothing has changed.

In 1970 I became an environmental activist. I was on final approach over Ahous Point to land on the hard sands of Ahous Bay when I saw that the forest of ancient trees and home to one of the oldest Indian settlements on the West Coast had been replaced with logging equipment.

One of the joys of coming here was to walk into the silence of this small forest of thousand-year-old spruce. That silence was now shattered by the sound of the chainsaw. On my return I phoned my friend Len Lauk who at that time was producing the CBC–TV news program, *The Seven O'Clock Show*. He gave me a cameraman and we flew back to document the destruction.

The result was a stern letter to me from Ray Williston, then Minister of Forests, on the importance of logging to B.C.'s economy and how everything I enjoyed, including my teaching position at University of B.C., depended on the logging industry.

The logs from the 1970 cutting were boomed in the bay, but before they could be towed to the mill, a storm came up and scattered them the length of the bay, where they remain to this day, buried in sand.

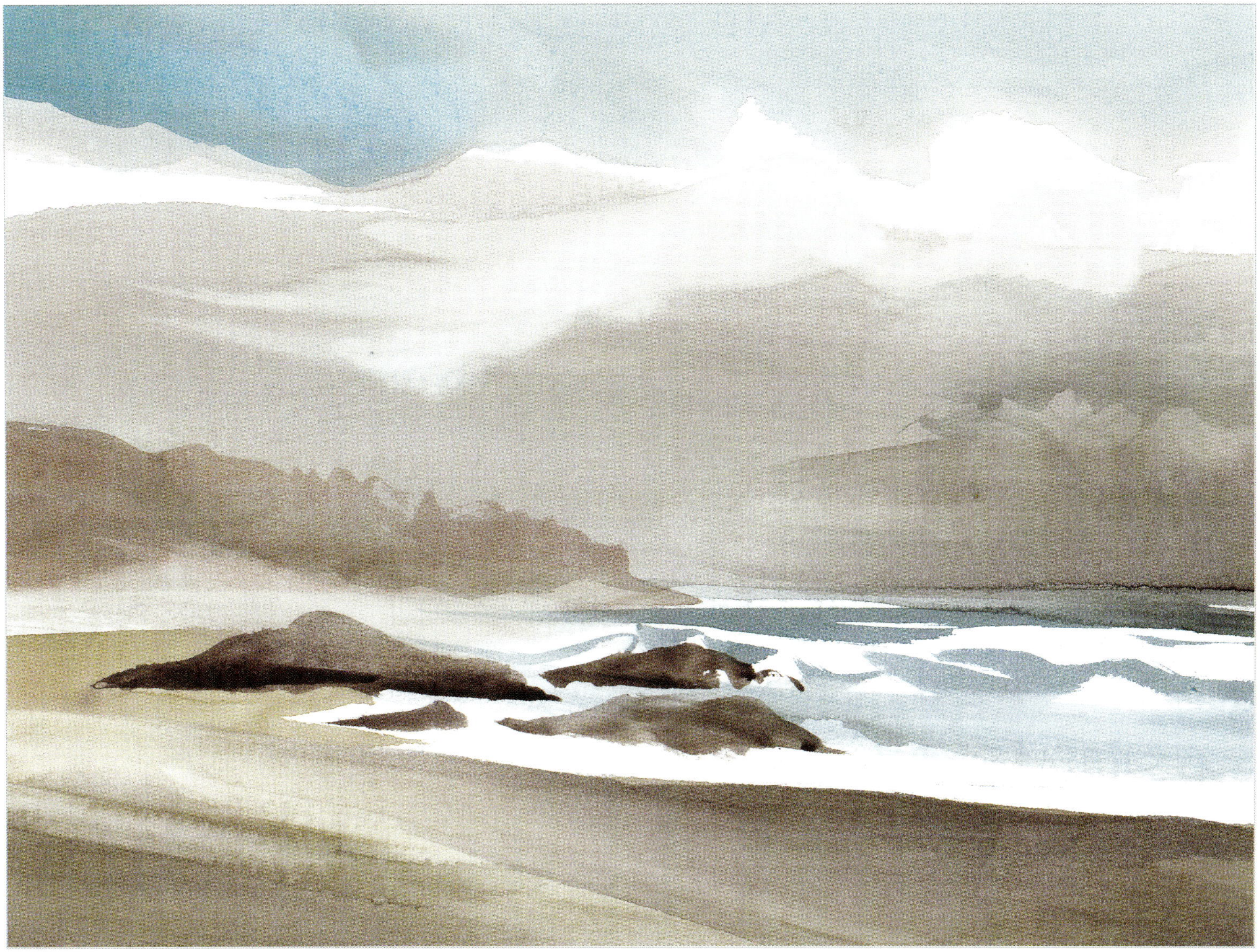

Chesterman Beach, West Coast, Vancouver Island, 17 June 1997

FLUTE AND PICCOLO PEAKS

WHISTLER MOUNTAIN

My fear of mountains and my love of them coexist. The capricious nature of wind and weather is what draws me into the mountains with my watercolours, but it is also what makes them dangerous for even the most experienced pilot.

The mountains almost cost me my life when I crashed my ski-plane into a glacial crevasse in 1983. John Reeves, the Toronto photographer renowned for his portraits of artists and writers, had been commissioned by CP Air's in-flight magazine to do a photo essay about me – "The Flying Artist" or some such title!

On September 7 of that year we flew up to the highest glacier in the Whistler area, the Cheakamus, at 8,000 feet, to do some painting and photography. When it was time to leave, the winds were gusting – one minute calm, the next up to forty knots, not unusual in the mountains – and the snow was wet and sticky, which would slow the takeoff run down the face of the glacier.

I waited for the winds to die, then started my first run, but I couldn't get up to speed because of the snow. I chopped power and taxied back up the slope for a second try. My first tracks were packed ice by then, so I expected to reach takeoff speed easily. I waited for the winds to drop again, then fired off, holding in my previous tracks. When I reached the end of them, I pulled on full flaps to "pop" the plane off the ground, but nothing happened.

I looked out and saw fine snow blowing along the surface of the glacier in the direction we were going. I realized that the wind had risen again, killing the lift my wings should have had. It was too late to stop and turn around. My only option was to maintain power to try to leap the 50-foot-wide crevasse ahead of us and land back on the glacier without sliding into the next crevasse.

I held power and we leapt the first abyss, crashing gently into a narrow crevasse that ran perpendicular to the main crevasse in the direction of our descent. It formed the stem of a T immediately across from where we had jumped the broad crevasse and was just wide enough to hold the body of the plane while supporting the wings. This minimized the impact of the crash, while preventing us from sliding on into the next crevasse. Six feet to the right or the left and we would have smashed into the ice.

I would like to say that this was a magnificent piece of flying, but the truth is that I had lost control. An invisible hand had pushed us into the only place that could have stopped our fall and cradled us through the long night on the edge of oblivion, waiting anxiously for the rescue by helicopter that finally came the next morning.

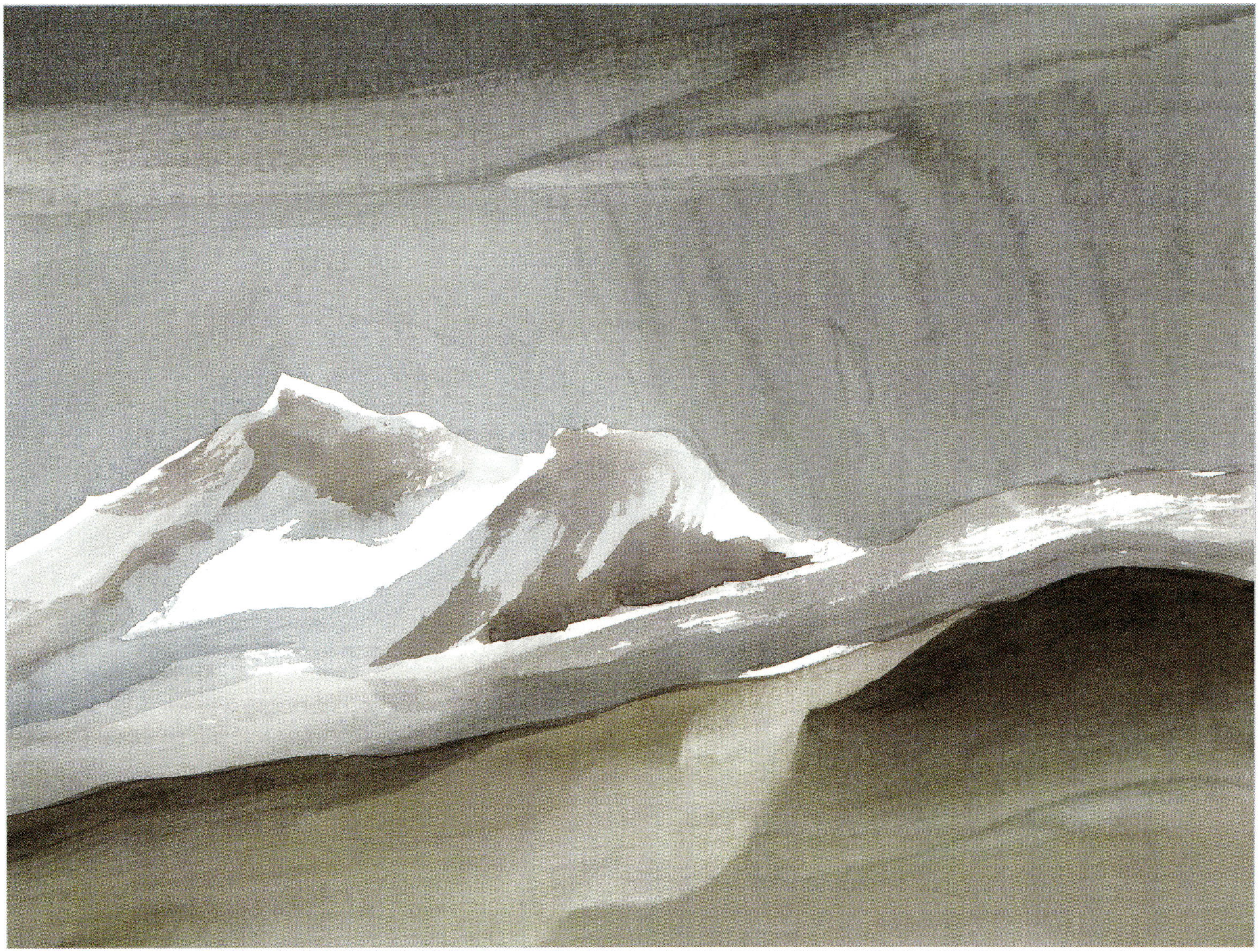

Flute and Piccolo Peaks, Whistler Mountain, 12 August 1996

GREAT GLACIER

STIKINE RIVER

The dense forest along the banks of the Stikine obscures the Great Glacier and the glacial lake from view when canoeing. Unless you know exactly where to pull in to shore, you will miss a magical experience. My friends and I portaged with two canoes for about a mile through the forest to emerge at the emerald-green lake which was slowly filling with the cobalt-blue icebergs that calved continually from the wall of the Great Glacier.

The icebergs moved slowly and majestically, sometimes rolling silently. We canoed in and around them before I settled down on a little peninsula to do this watercolour. It was only later that I realized how dangerous it had been to canoe in and around moving icebergs, but we had been drawn like moths to a flame.

There will always be those among us who mistrust Nature and fear it is working against us. They will never learn to live with danger: their terrors are their own terrors; the abyss is their own abyss. These people are forever, in Rilke's words, in "a small room in which they keep walking back and forth."

But I believe that if we respect Nature it will not let us fall, it will not let us down. We are on a river of possibilities, with no fear of the inexplicable, a fear which impoverishes the lives of those who would dwell only on the banks where nothing happens. We move and sound the depths of our own being. We are not looking out of the window of a small room – we are outside and moving through a magnificent landscape.

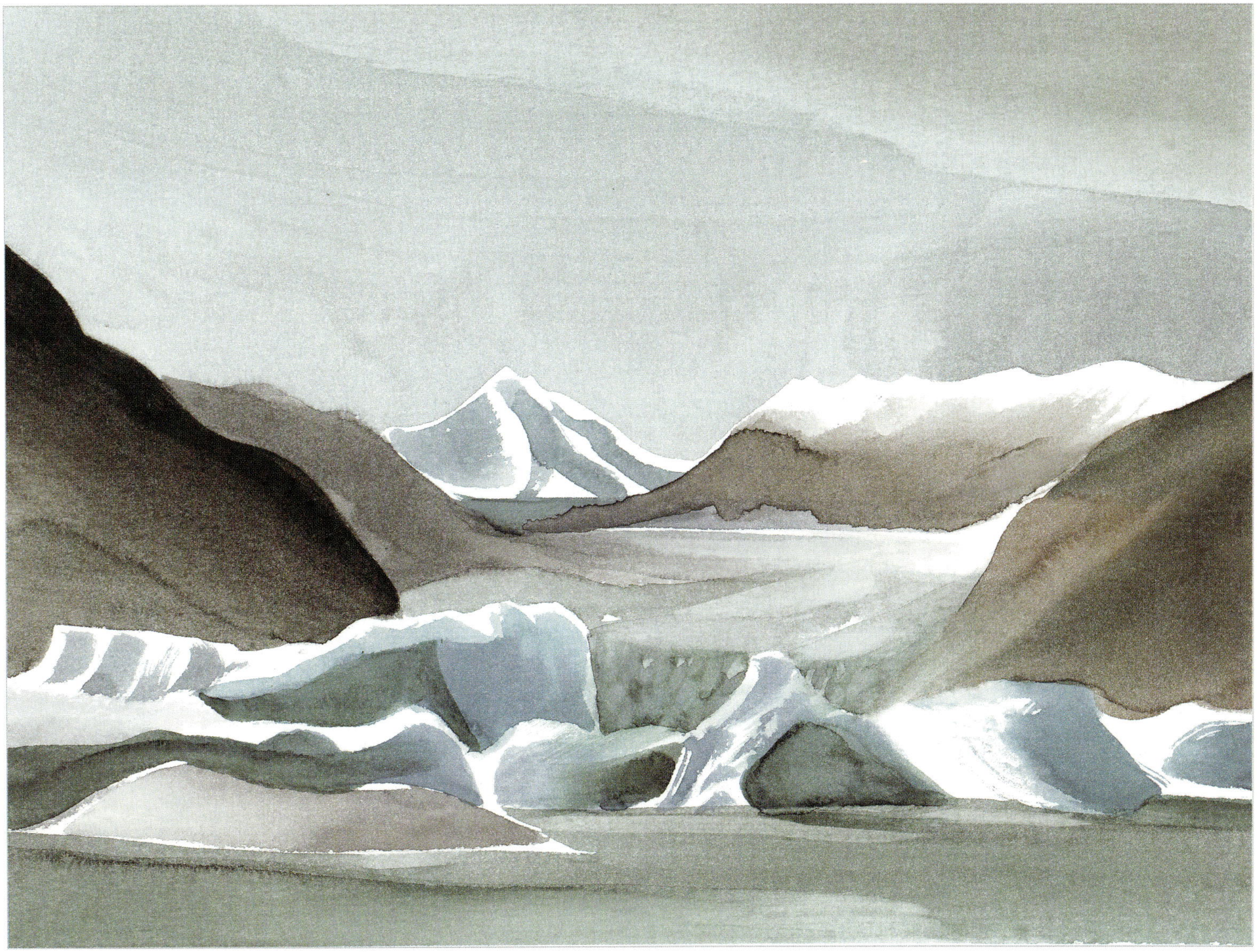

Great Glacier, Stikine River, 27 July 1996

BOUNDARY BAY

I hangar my flying boat at Delta Heritage Airpark on Boundary Bay. I have kept an airplane there for thirty years. It was little more than a farmer's field when I first landed there on 10 February 1968. I had just bought my Champion Sky-Trac in Penticton and was bringing it home. I was a thirty-five-hour wonder, attempting to land on a grass strip which from the air looked impossibly short. I must have circled the strip a dozen times, until the decision to land was made for me. I was almost out of gas.

Today Delta Airpark is home to a wonderful collection of Second World War "warbirds," as well as to the Recreational Aircraft Association / Canada, which has a workshop, hangar and clubhouse. We have a pilots' briefing room-cum-restaurant and four T-hangars full of lovingly cared for airplanes. Today the taxiways are paved. The one runway is still grass and still short to the inexperienced pilot. I love a soft, forgiving grass runway. Delta has the last grass strip in the Lower Mainland.

As the old saying goes, "There are old pilots and bold pilots, but there are no old, bold pilots." My fellow pilots at Delta are mostly "old" pilots, many Second World War veterans who found their love of flying in the old days when sex was safe and flying was dangerous. Over the years my hangar has housed my Champ, my Lake Buccaneer and my Polish Wilga 104 ski-plane,

On the day this watercolour was painted, my mechanic was working on my airplane. Frustrated at not being able to fly out to the islands, I took my watercolours over the dike, sat on a log and did this painting, looking towards Point Roberts.

It justified a day which would have otherwise been lost.

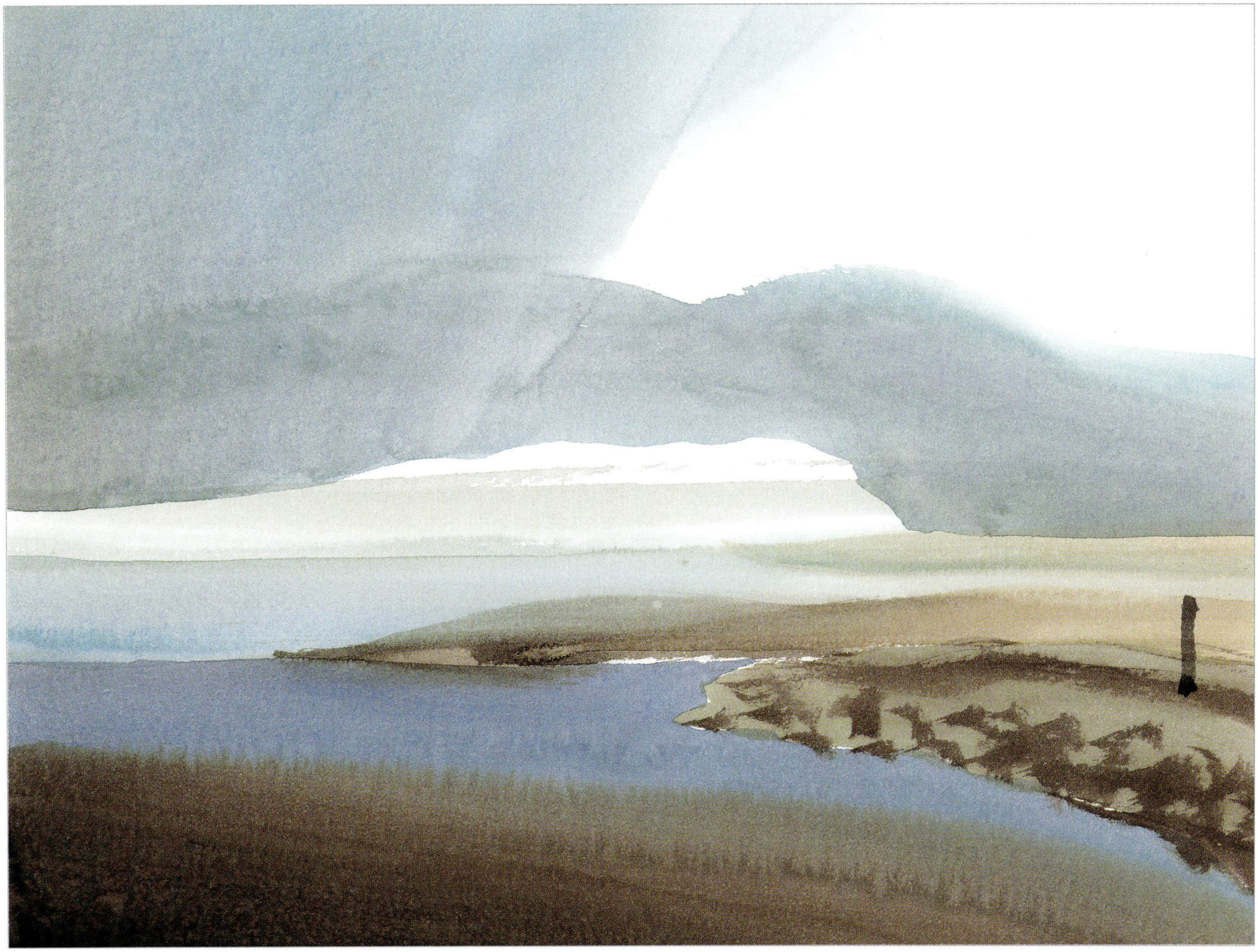

Boundary Bay, 9 February 1995

KUPER ISLAND

Kuper Island is across Houstoun Passage from Saltspring Island. I was on Tent Island looking across to Kuper Island when I painted this watercolour. It was a day of ever-changing seascapes around the Gulf Islands. It was a day that had the power to transform the view into a mystery of its own religion.

What I look at is a trigger for something else, something I bring to the landscape. I'm constantly making choices, even as the brush moves across the paper, because the brush is such a big, sloppy thing that I am half in and half out of control of it. I can have disasters or I can have very happy accidents. I have to be in the right frame of mind so that I can recognize these accidents when they happen.

I live for those moments when I experience a Zen-like oneness of Nature, hand and brush. And I relive those moments every time I meditate on the paintings that came out of them.

I am constantly striving to maintain a beneficial state of ignorance, knowing that if I ever realize fully with my conscious mind exactly how an effect is produced, I am doomed to the making of replicas.

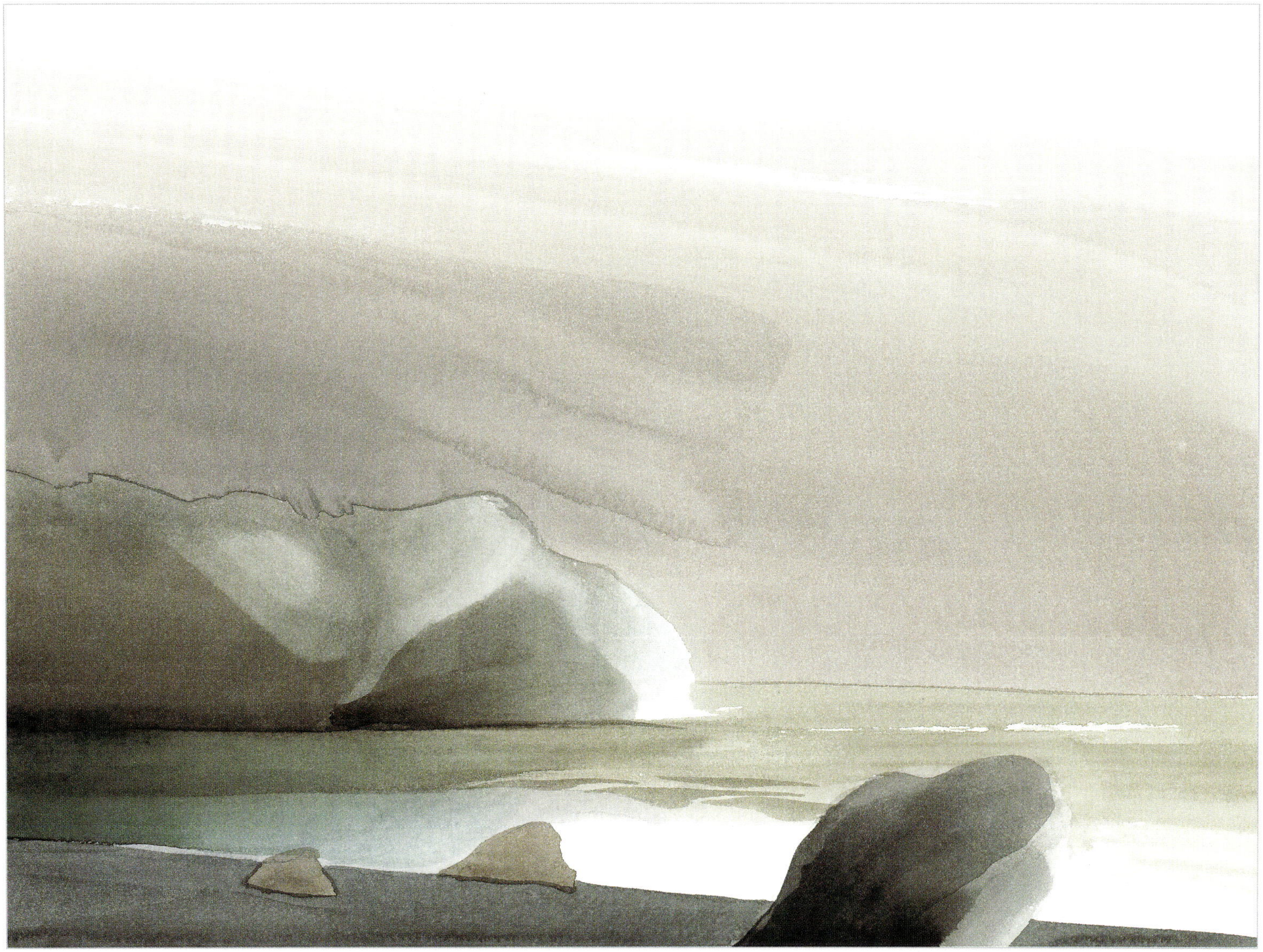

Rocks, Kuper Island, 14 May 1995

STIKINE RIVER

On a canoe trip from Telegraph Creek to Wrangell Island, Alaska, there were sixteen of us, including two guides. We had six tandem canoes and a large voyager canoe for our supplies. Three of my new friends were from France, three from the U.S.A. and eight from other parts of Canada. I was the only one from British Columbia. Our wilderness looms large in the minds of those who do not live here. They know that we in B.C. are the custodians of some of the last wild places on earth.

Six days into the canoe trip, we camped on a sand bar. The waters of this little creek were warm enough for me to plunge in with a bar of soap before spreading out my watercolours to do this painting of the clear air of a broad and expansive valley.

I remember the fine, damp sand where my footprints intermingled with the fresh prints of a grizzly bear, and I remember being glad not to be alone.

On more than one occasion, I have shared my painting spot with grizzly bears. Painting along the Tatshenshini, the largest denning area for grizzlies in the world, it was a rare day that I was painting out of sight of them. They grazed the river bank like sheep as we drifted by.

Once when painting in the Cariboo, at the mouth of a creek flowing into Chilko Lake, I sensed a presence behind me. I turned to see four large grizzlies standing on hind legs, sniffing the air. They cannot see very far but can smell for miles. I quietly packed up my watercolours and left the bears to what was obviously their fishing spot.

I have painted in the home of fifty grizzly bears, at Khutzeymateen Inlet near Prince Rupert. At low tide, they came down to graze on the intertidal sedgegrass. With a dozen or so grizzlies, some only fifty feet away, I painted. They knew I was there but were ignoring me. However, in case one of them decided to be an art critic, I kept a 12-gauge shotgun beside me.

Once when I was anchored near the shore of a lake, a moose stuck his head, antlers and all, into the open canopy of my flying boat, dribbling moose drool all over the pilot's seat.

To date I have been lucky with animals in the wild; I have simply enjoyed them.

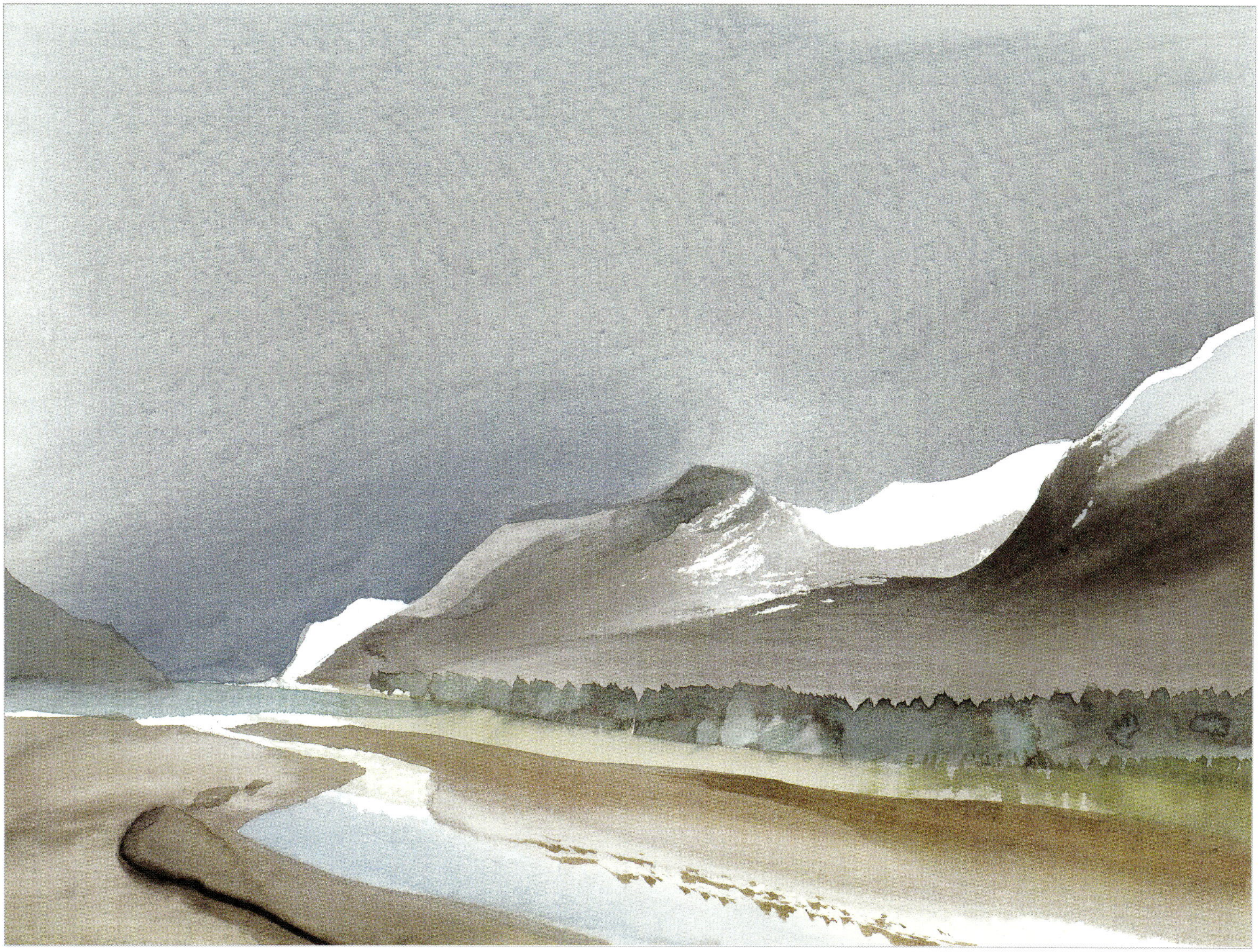

Camp 6, Stikine River, 27 July 1996

TATSHENSHINI RIVER

SEDIMENTS CREEK

The Tat has provided me with some of the best landscape British Columbia has to offer. In 1992, my friend Neil Hartling of Nahanni River Adventures, invited me to join him, his guides and a group of hardened river men and women to raft down the Tatshenshini. The valley at that time was in danger of being lost to mining interests.

True to the north, my companions all had names that told you something about them. Like Whiskey John, Blasphemous Bill, Denver Jim, Rifleman Al, the Iron Dutchman, Chilkoot Max, Yellowknife Lydia and Evelyn the Tease. And let me not forget Blind Euclid. Because of his skill and independence, I did not realize he was blind until four days into our voyage. I later learned that he was the president and the CEO of the Canadian National Institute for the Blind and president of the World Blind Union. Over the intervening years our friendship has evolved from this chance encounter in the wilderness.

We were all on a spiritual quest, through a land under threat of exploitation before the mountains were even named. The next year I faxed a letter to B.C. premier Mike Harcourt asking him to protect this wilderness:

Dear Mr. Premier / Mike:

I spent last summer rafting and painting the Tatshenshini and Alsek Rivers. It is without a doubt one of the greatest wilderness river areas on this planet. In this place where I watched a thriving grizzly bear population grazing undisturbed, it is heartbreaking for me to think of giant ore trucks roaring down the valley every ten minutes for the next 25 years.

A wild Tat is a resource forever. We in B.C. are custodians of some of the most spectacular landscape that this world has to offer and the Tatshenshini heads the list for me. Wilderness and mining cannot co-exist. I am leaving for the Yukon June 18th to once again experience this wild and wonderful country. I will mine it for paintings – watercolours I hope will be around long after the mining companies have taken their profits and left, leaving us with acid and heavy-metal-filled tailing ponds to seep into the Tat and Alsek Rivers.

There can be no compromise here. Good luck and best wishes for the hard choices.

Toni

Today, thanks to the actions of Mike Harcourt and others, this vast area has been preserved and has also been designated a World Heritage Site by the United Nations.

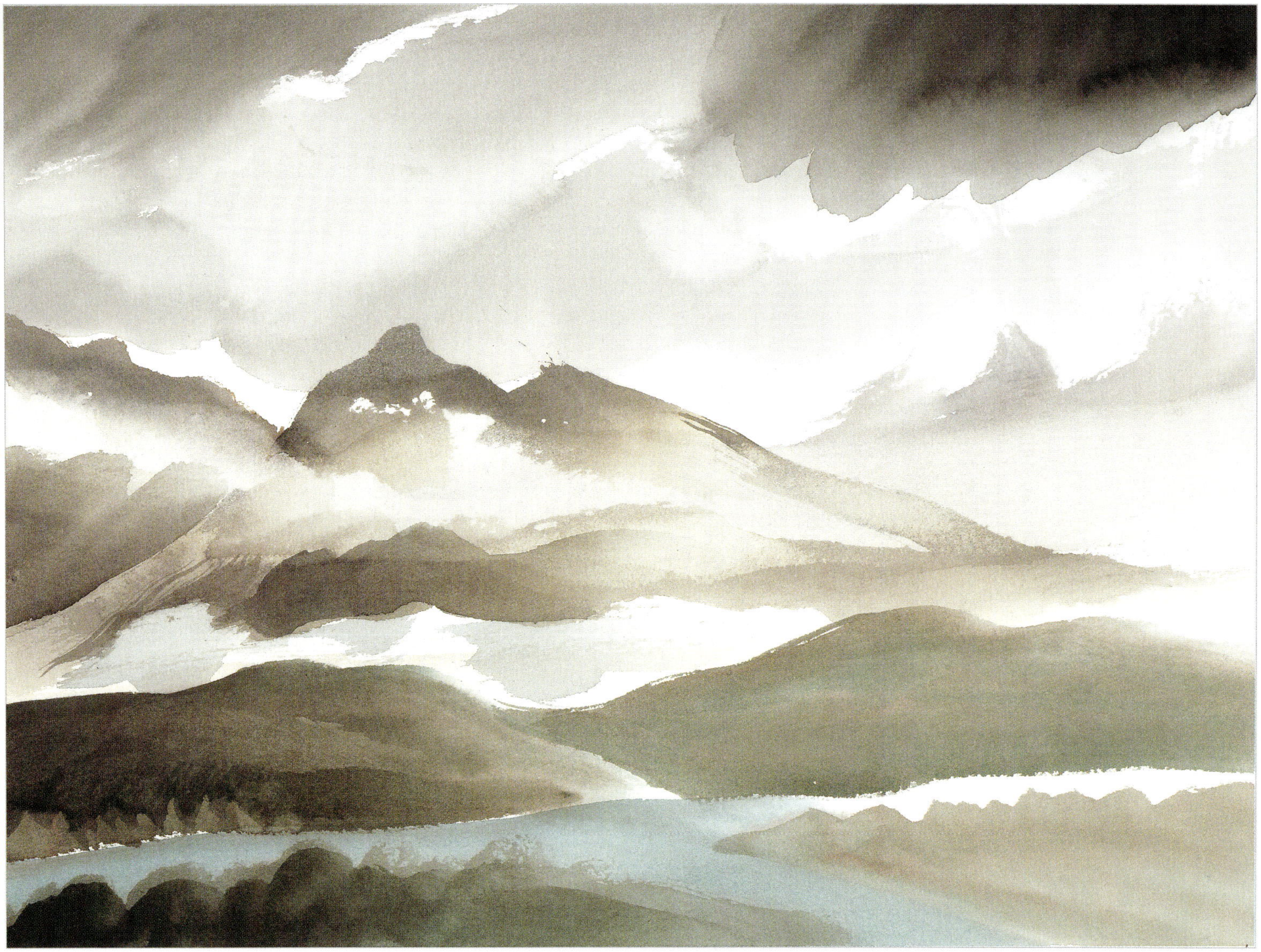

Camp Four, across the Tatshenshini River at Sediments Creek, 27 July 1992

MUNSEN MOUNTAIN

PENTICTON

For two short years in the 1950s Penticton was my home. I still look on it as my hometown in British Columbia, a place I return to time after time. My mother and one of my sisters still live there. Every time I visit, I paint a few watercolours, and many of these watercolours I have donated to the South Okanagan Art Gallery.

I made a living in Penticton as an architectural draftsman and by giving art lessons on the side. I did this for two years before deciding in 1957 to move to Mexico, then the cheapest place in North America, to buy the time I needed to develop as an artist.

For the next three years I devoted myself to painting full time, returning to Canada only when sales were sufficient for me to afford my own country on my own terms, as an artist. Mexico served another purpose. I was a single parent with two young daughters, and domestic help was affordable there.

Penticton has changed little since the 1950s. Once the available land between Lake Okanagan and Skaha Lake had been used up, there was little space for expansion, a limitation that has saved the town. I can still walk down Main Street, visiting shopkeepers who remember me and my parents. My old apartment building, "Lake Shore Manor," is exactly as it was in 1955. Only I have changed.

The white light of early morning still bathes the valley and the wind still comes up in the afternoon, making my flight back to Vancouver a bumpy one. I know all the passes and alternate routes between the Okanagan Valley and Hope, so I can pick my way through the mountains in poor weather and arrive home safely.

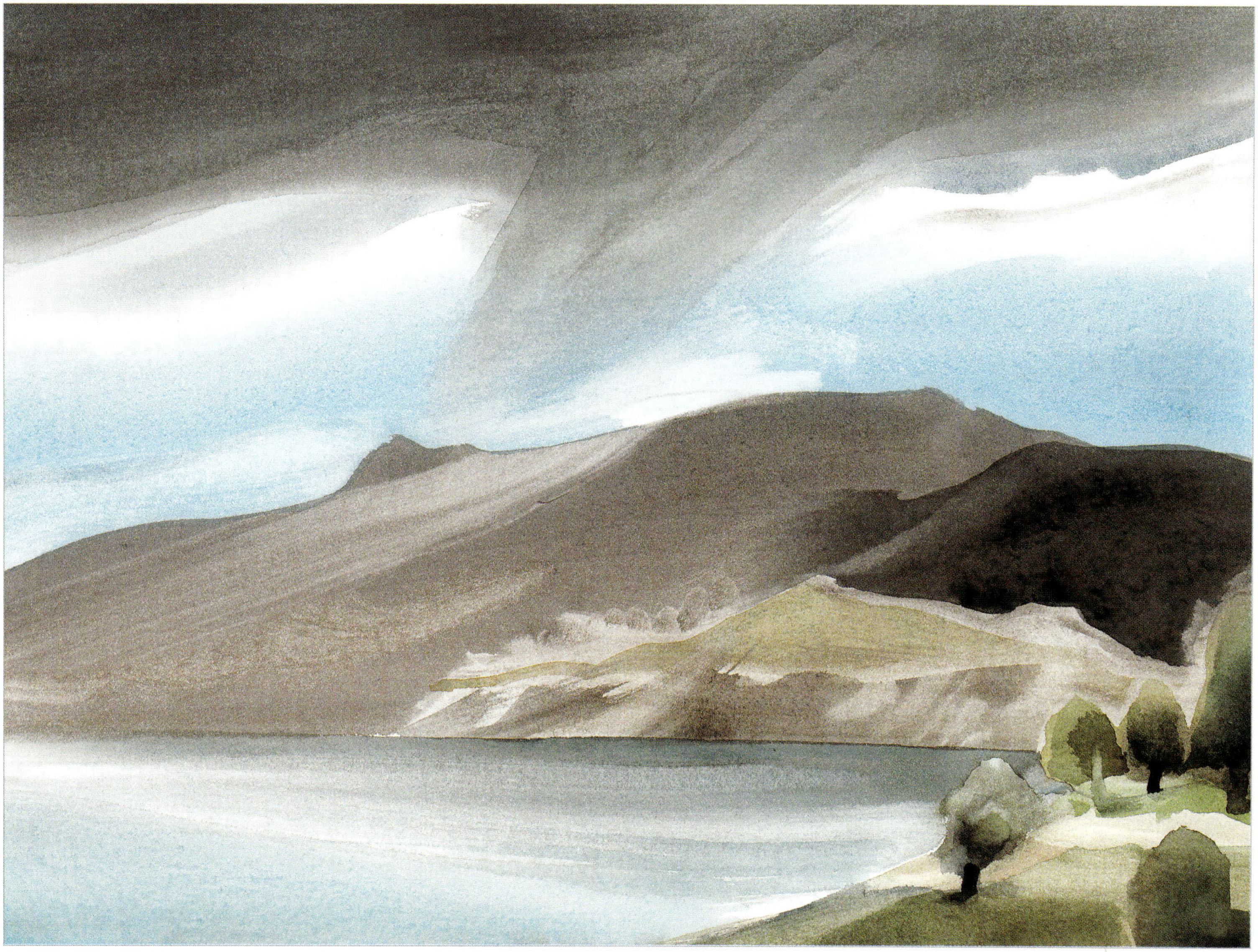

Morning Shower, Munsen Mountain, Penticton, 21 August 1997

WALKER HOOK

SALTSPRING ISLAND

Each of these watercolours holds memories for me. Not knowing Walker Hook was a nudists' beach, I taxied my amphibious flying boat out onto the sand. The nudists kept a discreet distance, allowing me to paint.

Despite the distraction, I sat on the beach all afternoon and did five watercolours. Instead of moving around myself, I often just look around me in all directions and select different views to paint. On this occasion, that seemed to be an appropriate way to deal with the landscape.

When I was about to leave, I discovered that the wheels of my amphibian had become stuck in the sand. Whereupon a dozen nudists ran down the beach and pushed me off. I met one of my saviours a week later on Georgia Street, an attractive young lady in a sharp business suit, all smiles and amused that I did not recognize her.

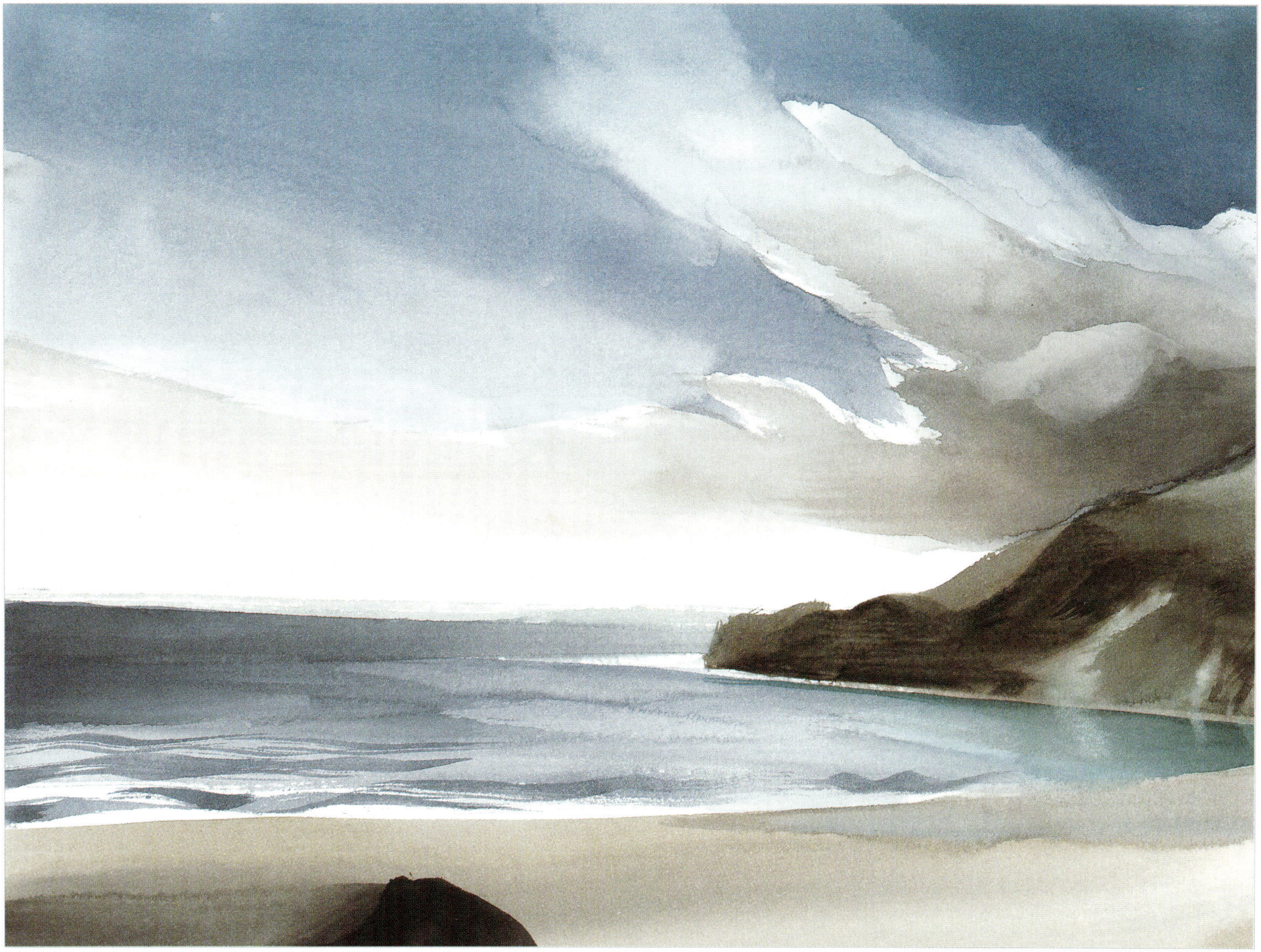

Walker Hook, Saltspring Island, 6 August 1994

HATZIC ROCK

MISSION

Hatzic Rock is the site of an ancient settlement occupied by the ancestors of the Stõ:lõ. The oral history of the Stõ:lõ people has it that respected leaders were transformed into great stones like Hatzic Rock. I painted this rock shortly after archeologists from the Stõ:lõ nation and the University of British Columbia discovered this site.

Research has uncovered tens of thousands of artifacts and remains of the earliest dwelling structures known in British Columbia. The settlement has been occupied by the Stõ:lõ for as long as 9,000 years, pre-dating ancient Egypt by 4,000 years and making the Stone Age burial circles on my native Isle of Man look like recent history, along with Stonehenge, which is a mere 2,000 years old.

There is a mystery to these age-old monuments. I am drawn to them in the hope that a little of their spiritual presence will find its way into my watercolours.

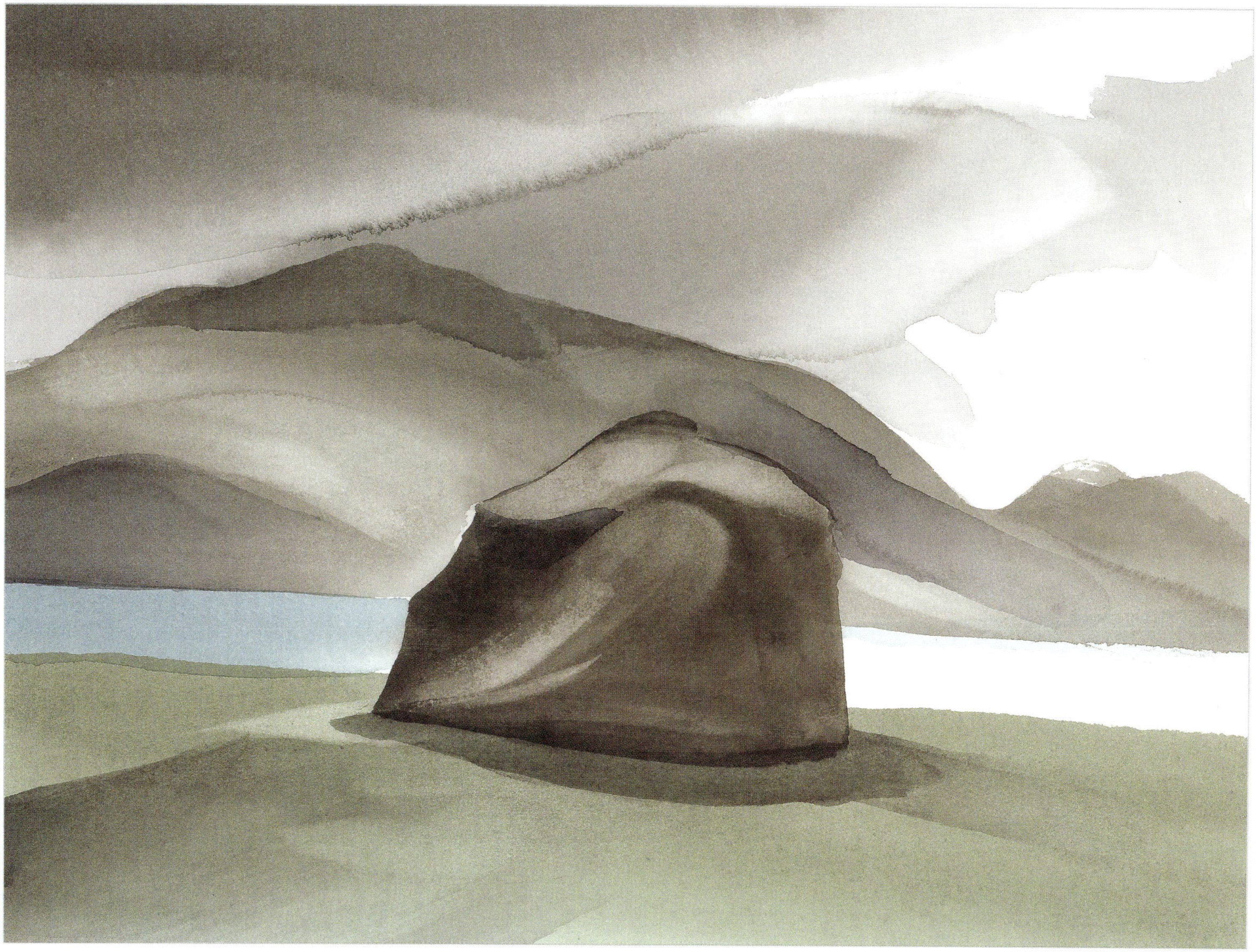

Hatzic Rock, Mission, 4 September 1991

STANLEY PARK

VANCOUVER

I was asked by a school teacher friend if I would take her special class of attention-deficit, hyperactive, dyslectic children on a painting trip. I identify with such children because I was a little bit that way myself as a child. The school system often fails such children. I took this unruly lot to Stanley Park on a wet and windy day.

On this occasion, there was no attention deficit. The rain was ignored as they watched me produce a rain-splashed watercolour. I asked them if they could gather some sticks and light a small fire on the beach, so I could dry my watercolour. I have yet to see such eager cooperation among children with an adult. For them it was a "spot in time" to be always remembered, I could tell.

As a child, I painted constantly. I would not go out to play like other children. I was criticized by friends and family for it, but I was a stubborn child. I have a more generous spirit today, but I am still stubborn about my work. Some would call it dedication.

Encouragement is most important. I had just enough of it and also just enough discouragement to push against. I put great faith in negative reactions, it helps us define our purpose.

I did, however, achieve a certain status at school. It was during the Second World War, and my ability to draw realistic pictures of both Allied and enemy war planes excited admiration among my peers, giving me a sense of worth which I enjoyed.

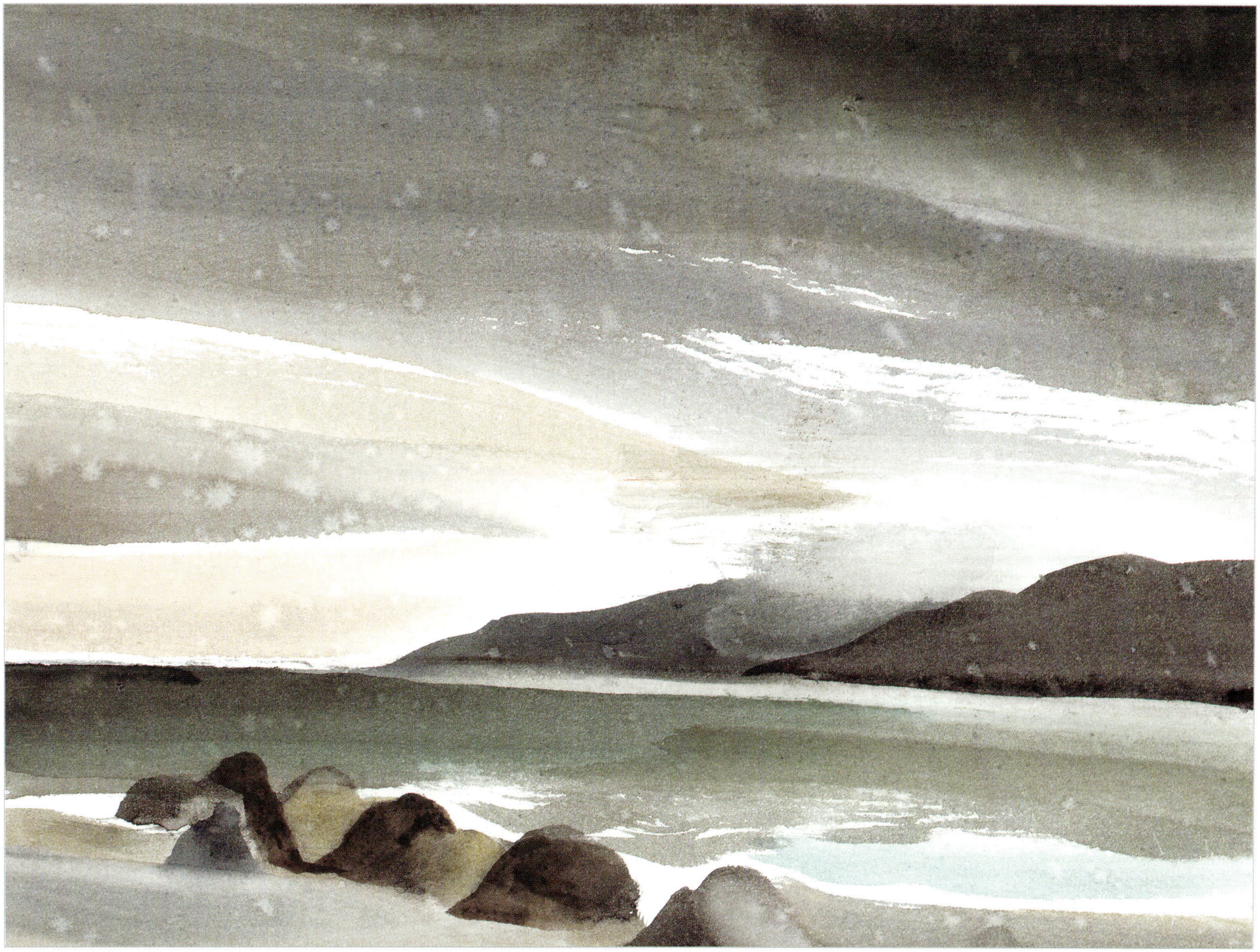

Second Beach, Stanley Park, Vancouver, 23 June 1997

PARADISE RANCH BAY

LAKE OKANAGAN

This is one of my favourite spots on the lake and the childhood home of my friend, the film director Sandy Wilson. It was here that she made *My American Cousin*. The present owner invited me to stay in her guest cottage, give a watercolour class to a few friends and do some painting myself. It was a wonderful social occasion, and on top of that I could take my flying boat directly from Vancouver to this bay on the lake in just one hour.

I have not taught formally for many years but enjoy giving a workshop once or twice a year. I have observed that students often make up their minds beforehand exactly what they're going to do, which doesn't take into account all the happy accidents that can happen en route. Often I'll see a student in the middle of a painting with things going ever so well. I'll hold my breath and not say a thing. When I come back half an hour later, they've painted over everything I thought was great.

That's the result of holding in your mind a fixed image of what you think you want at the end of the day. There is no room for the journey. Painting is a journey and you always have to be in a position to take side-roads. Or to totally change your mind or turn everything upside down or go backwards.

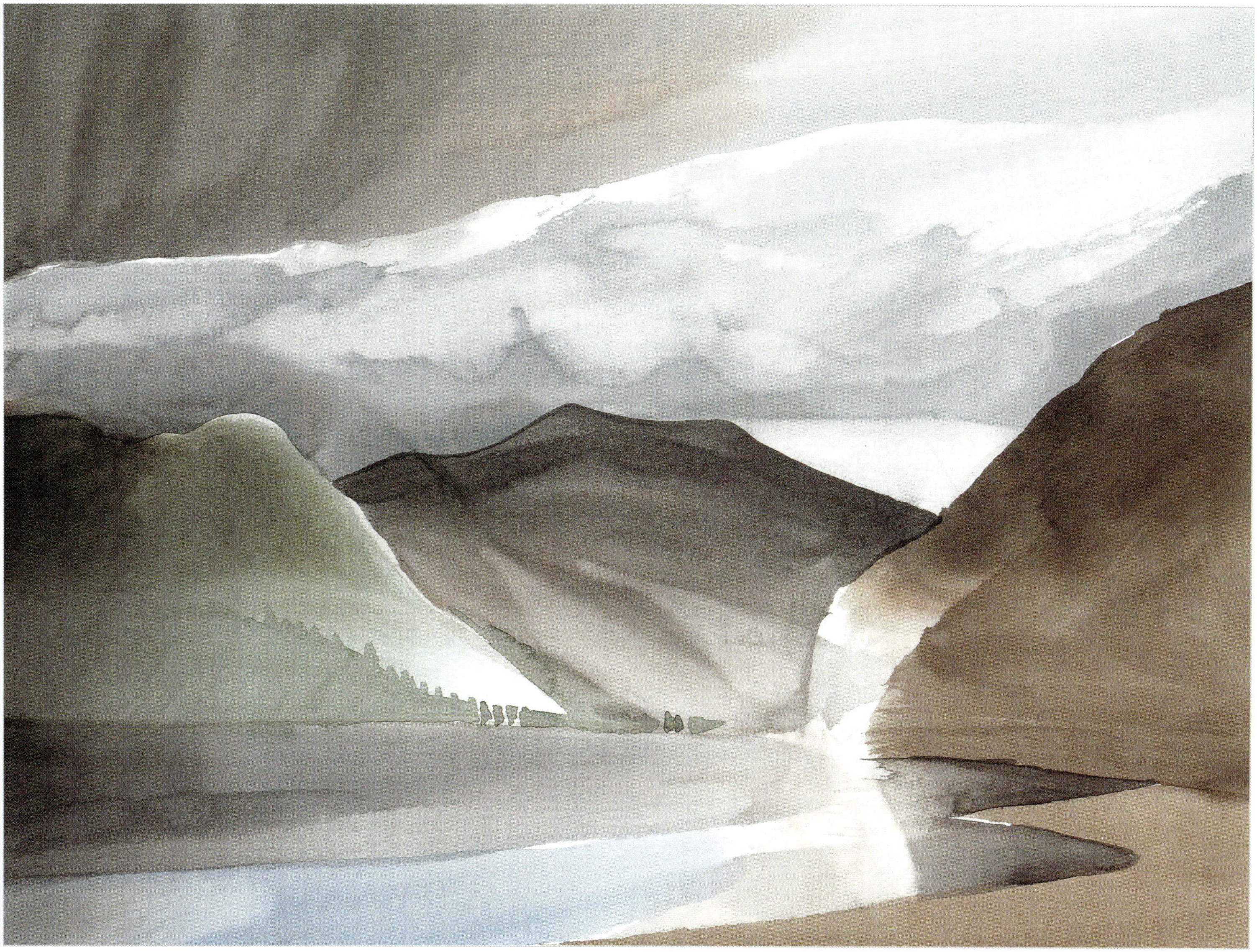

Paradise Ranch Bay, Lake Okanagan, 17 June 1995

HEADWATERS OF THE STEIN RIVER

I was doing a pilot report for an aviation magazine on a new STOL (short takeoff and landing) seaplane called a Bushmaster. It was an opportunity to take my watercolours into some of the small jewel-like lakes above the Stein Valley that until now I could only overfly in my bigger flying boat.

Unlike Stein Lake, which is dark green and mysterious, these lakes are a pure ultramarine blue. This watercolour is of Elton Lake on the southwest ridge of the Stein watershed. The mountains rising out of this lake were the colour of rusty iron, a dark burnt sienna, and by contrast made the blue of the lake appear even more intense.

In the summer of 1988, conflict between environmentalists and logging interests in the Stein Valley was heating up. Paul George of the Western Canada Wilderness Committee informed me that the Committee was $35,000 in the red. I suggested taking a group of fellow artists into Stein Lake to paint, then holding an art sale of the resulting works, thereby achieving two goals: retiring the Committee's debt and drawing attention to the plight of the Stein. We were successful on both counts.

Two years later, Chief Perry Redon, then chairman of the Lillooet Tribal Council, flew me by helicopter into the west end of Stein Lake to paint a watercolour which could be made into a poster to raise money for the development of the Lytton and Mount Currie Indian People's Stein Valley Cultural Centre. While I was painting, Chief Redon beat his drum and sang to the four quarters of the Earth. I was inspired, and soon we had a watercolour for the Stein poster.

Later we flew up to a cave high on a cliff on the north bank of the Stein, a place once used for spirit training. A boy or a girl would spend the night alone in this cave, singing and dancing before a fire. At daybreak, aided by the spirit of the Dawn, they had a dream or vision in which their individual spirit helper appeared and gave them a song to be used throughout their life to invoke that spirit. This puberty ritual gave power to the individual, establishing a physical and psychological break with childhood.

I peered into the cave from the hovering helicopter and could see walls covered with red ochre paintings of dreams and visions. I particularly remember a large eagle, along with other birds and animals.

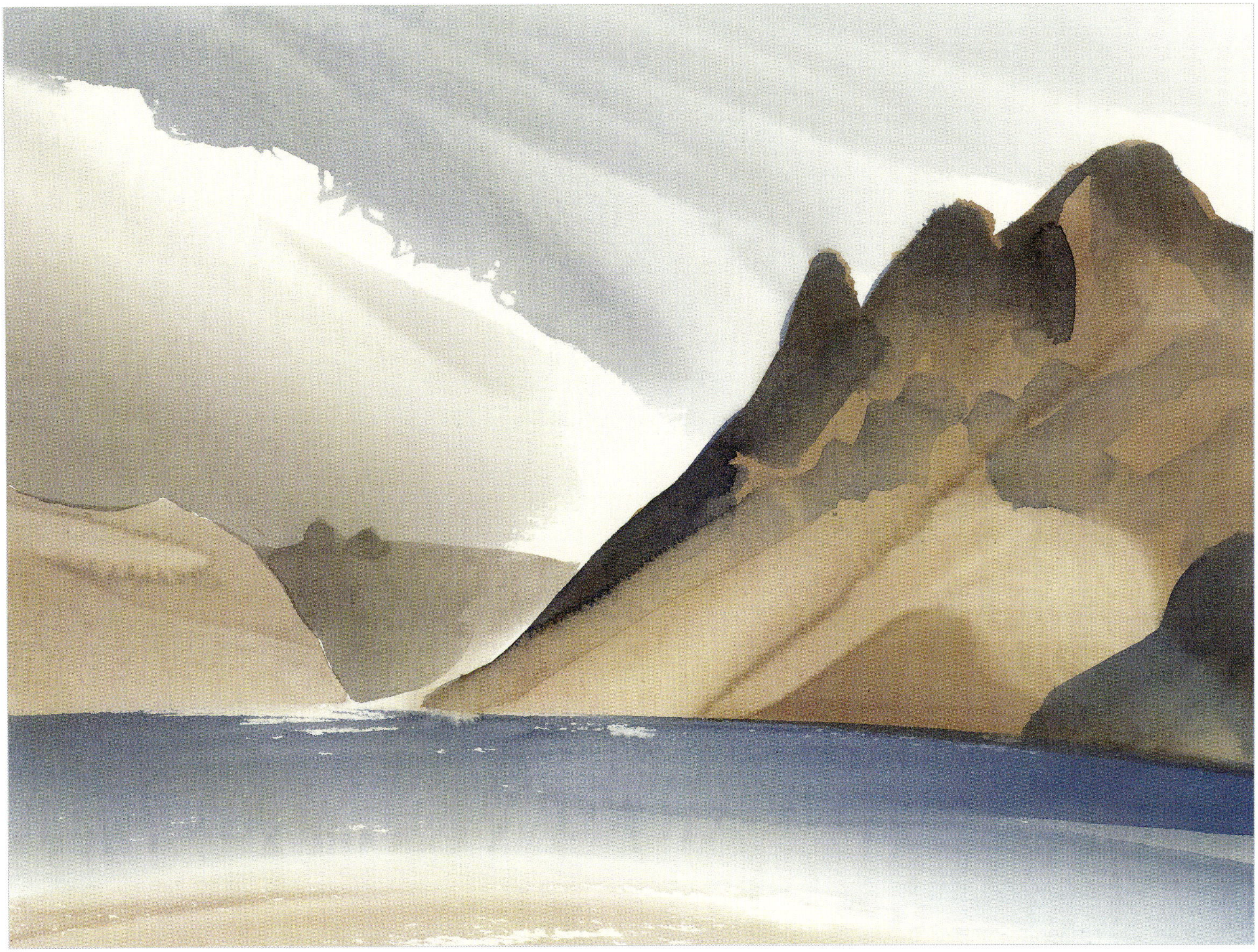

Headwaters of the Stein River, 30 August 1988

BOUNDARY BAY

There is no medium better suited to the capture of the evanescent moment than watercolour. With it and some skill, such a moments can be transformed into a permanent memorial to sun and wind-driven clouds.

John Constable made many studies of English skies for their own sake, responding directly to the fleeting moment. My old art teacher, John Hobbs Nicholson, would say when painting clouds, "Look and don't look back or you will turn into a pillar of crap."

In Asian art there is the Zen concept of the "beginner's mind," a sort of emptiness which allows the landscape to be painted, not by the artist, but *through* the artist.

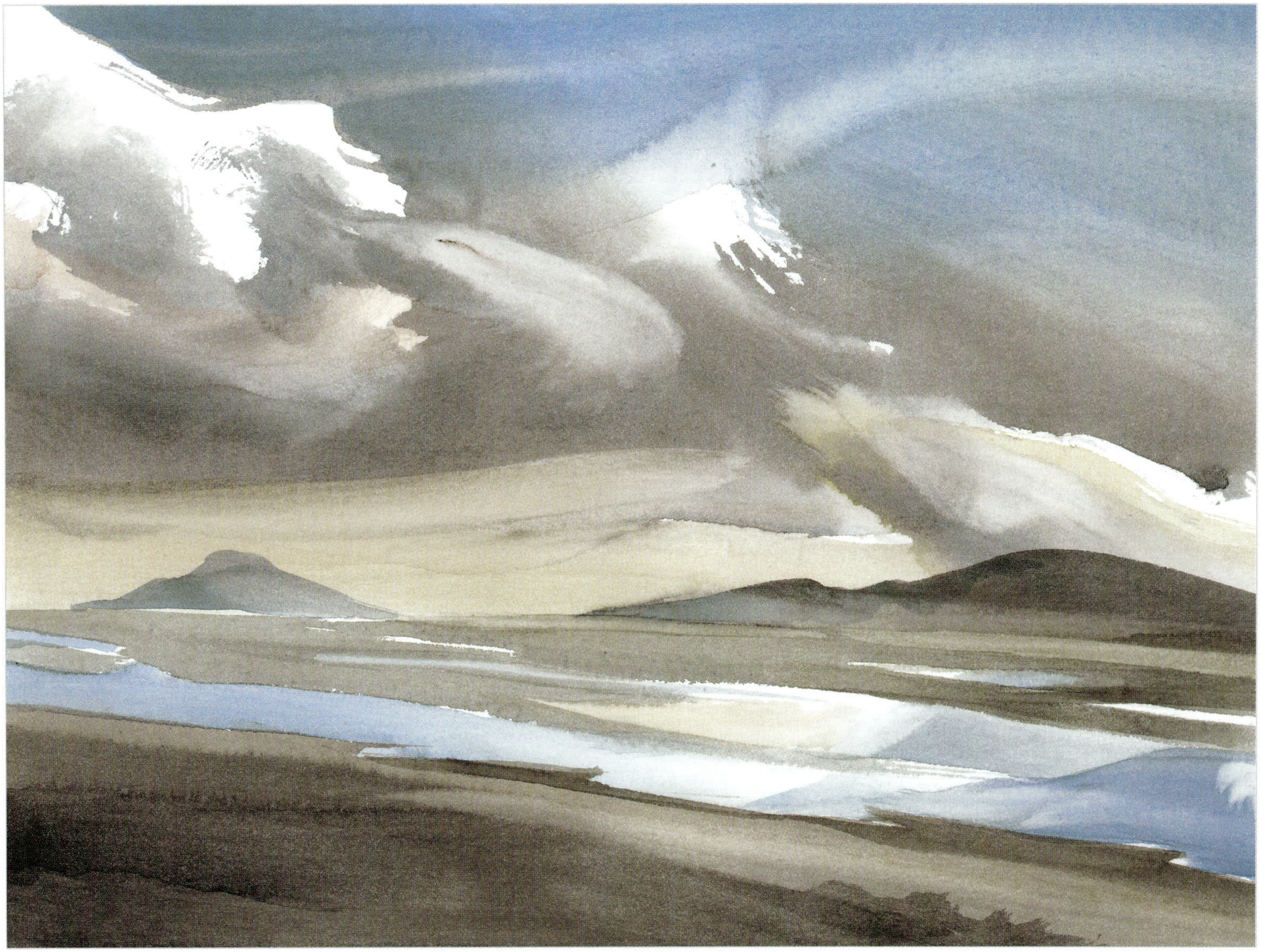

Boundary Bay, 1 May 1997

MT. BLANCHARD AND ALOUETTE MOUNTAIN

The solitude of the mountains often oppresses the spirits of those from east of the Rockies. Among my contemporaries in British Columbia, there are very few painters who choose the mountains as their subject. Yet it was the mountains that first drew me to this province and have kept me here ever since.

The mountains of Golden Ears Park above Pitt Lake are on the nearest freshwater lake, a scant fifteen minutes from my airpark in Delta. As a result, I probably spend more time painting among these mountains than any others.

My favourite lake in Golden Ears Park is Thomas Lake. It is mid-June before it is free enough of ice for me to land my flying boat. One spring I ran my amphibian into a snow bank at the end of the lake and jumped out onto the snow bank, only to discover that the snow was supported only by thin ice. I plunged through this ice into deep, freezing water.

Fortunately I was holding a rope attached to the airplane and was able to pull myself to the surface and get back into the cockpit. I turned on the heater and fired up the engine and flew out of there before I froze to death.

With little accidents like this occuring every once in a while, chances are I will not die in my studio from paint fumes.

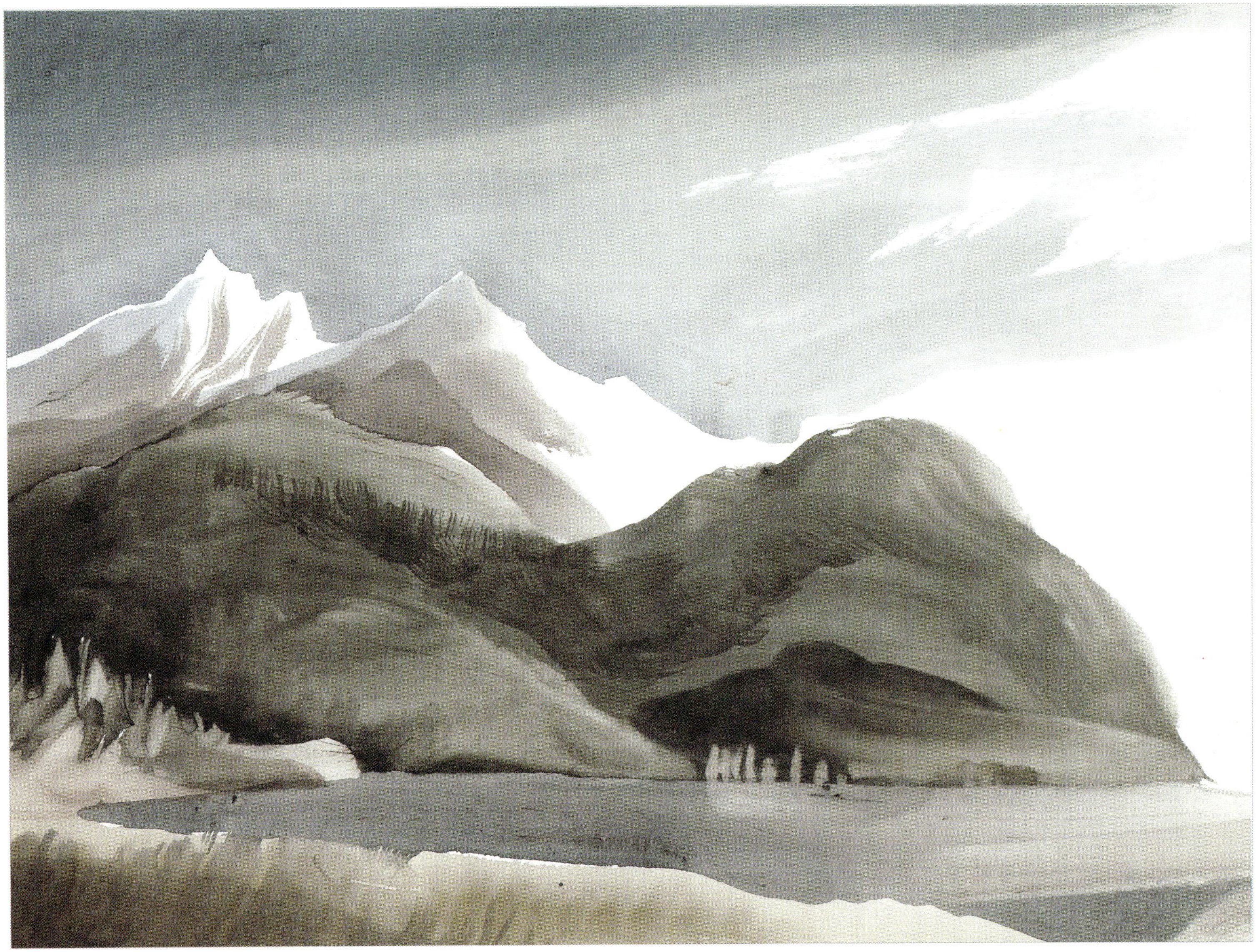

Mt. Blanchard and Alouette Mountain above Pitt River, 28 January 1994

BROWNING BAY

NORTH PENDER ISLAND

The Gulf Islands are small worlds unto themselves. Even though they seem to be strung together like pearls on a silken cord, each one has been through a unique evolution. Rock formations, ground cover and forests differ from island to island. I could never run out of subjects to paint among these islands on my doorstep.

Over the years I have done much painting on North and South Pender Islands. I often stop in at the restaurant on Bedwell Harbour, taxiing up onto the beach under the restaurant's balcony, much to the surprise of the guests who always ask the same questions: Where do you come from? How long is the flight? The answer is, "From Vancouver, in fifteen minutes." After a quick lunch, I taxi off to paint in one of the numerous coves on the bay.

This watercolour was painted above Browning Bay, where there is a field beside an orchard of old, gnarled apple trees. In cold weather, I can get out of the wind here and find shelter to paint. The restaurant there with home-cooked meals to warm up on makes it a good winter painting spot.

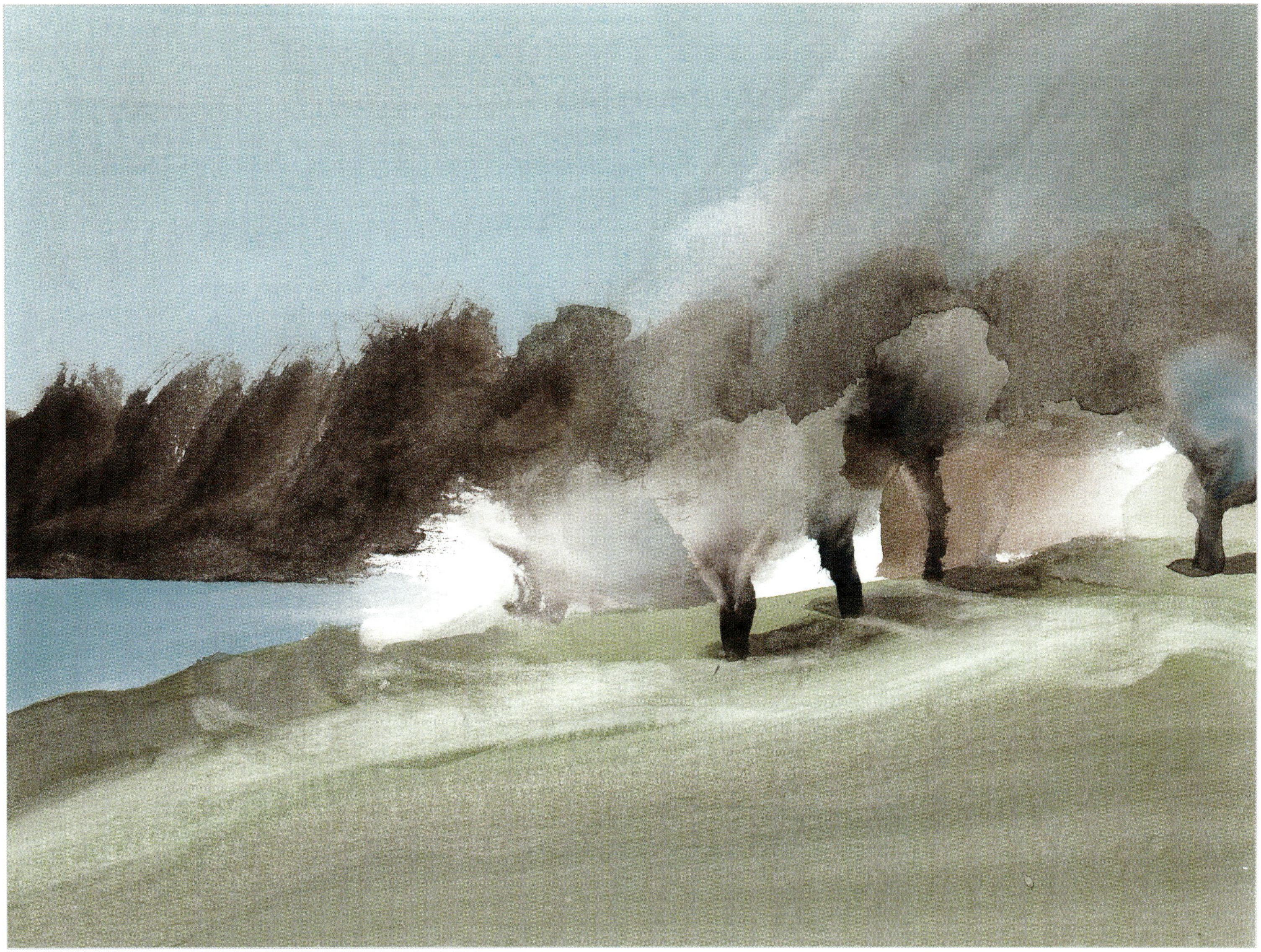

Old Orchard, Browning Bay, North Pender Island, 22 February 1997

PITT LAKE

I have watched sunsets around the world and, to me, ours on the British Columbia coast are the most dramatic, often suddenly bursting out after a long, gray, wet day.

On this late fall evening, I was flying along the North Shore mountains when the sky lit up. I put down on Pitt Lake. A light breeze was coming out of the sun. I let the flying boat weathercock into the wind and float gently backwards down the middle of the lake. I climbed out onto the wing and painted this watercolour in thirty minutes. The good watercolours take a lifetime – plus half an hour.

As the light faded, I was left with the bare bones of landscape: sky, rock and water. With an uncluttered mind and clear perception, I took off into the twilight of my own painting, homeward bound.

Matisse said, "It is the process whereby the artist incorporates the external world within himself, until the object becomes like part of his own being, until he has it within him . . . . It is the forms of the outer world which enrich the inner life. The inner life is not welter, but a shape of active seeing."

Van Gogh, in a letter to his brother, claims to "devour nature ceaselessly," and finds himself "in surroundings which entirely engross me, which so order, fix, regulate, renew and enlarge my thoughts that I am quite wrapped up in them."

Just as I was wrapped up in this sunset.

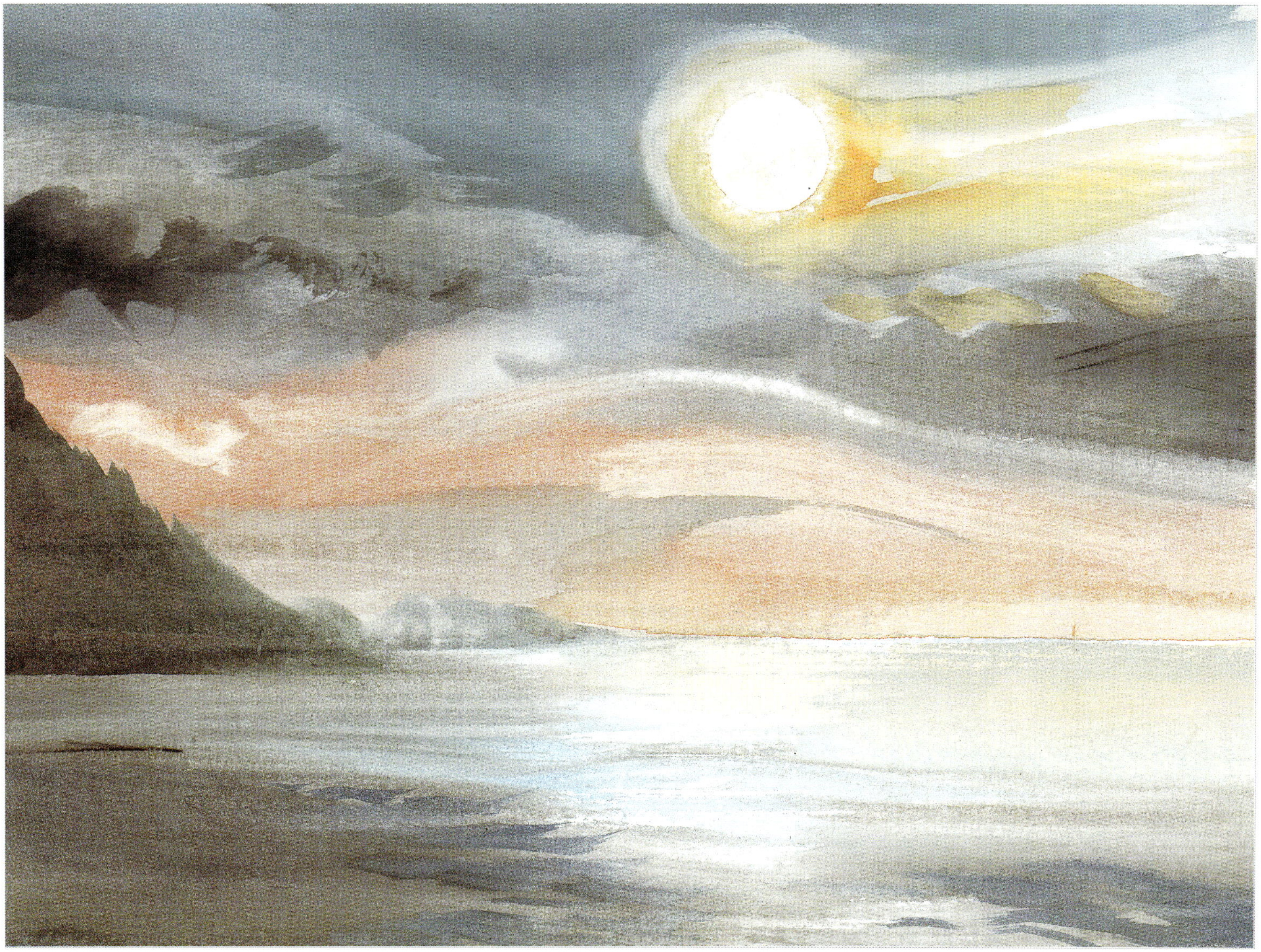

Sunset, Pitt Lake, 9 November 1996

SILVER STAR MOUNTAIN

Because I was not wearing skis, I had to talk the ski-lift operator into giving me a special dispensation to take my watercolours to the summit. If it were not for my determination, this watercolour and a few more I did that day would never have happened.

I found a perfect place to paint in the ski instructors' heated hut. I spread out my watercolours and paper on a table under a large window. The mountains were sharp in the thin, clear air. Before an audience of ski instructors, I did this painting.

One need not suffer to paint; in fact, suffering from cold and exhaustion robs one of the energy needed to concentrate. I learnt this early in life when I had cycled too far or climbed too high in search of subjects and in the process became too exhausted to paint.

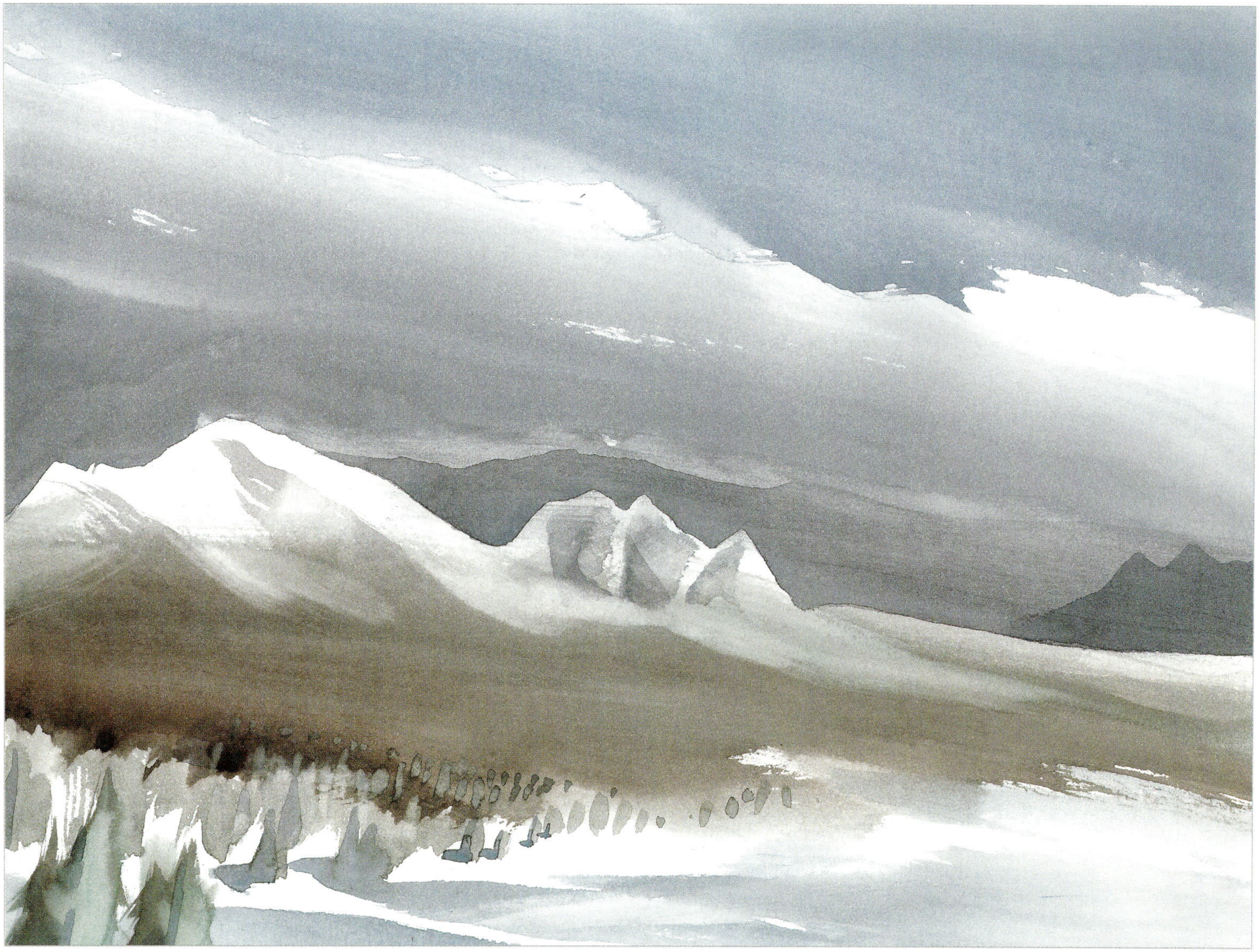

Silver Star Mountain, 25 March 1995

TUMBO CHANNEL

As a pilot, it is necessary that I study meteorology and look scientifically at clouds and what they are telling me, like the direction and force of the wind and whether I can expect a free ride on the wind up and over the mountains or if I will have to pick my way through the valleys searching for an updraft. On which side of the valley can I expect to find it? The clouds will tell me! They will tell me to stay on the ground or go flying. To expect a smooth ride or a bumpy one. The clouds will tell me.

At the same time I am an artist, observing the infinite and pursuing that elusive inner spirit found in the clouds. Riding the canyons and peaks in the tops of towering summer cumulus clouds is an exhilarating, even god-like, experience. Dipping a wing into a sharp-edged cumulus and pulling the vapour out like candy floss is a kind of cosmic playfulness known only to pilots. These are the flights that live in memory.

The early nineteenth-century classification of clouds into nimbus, stratus, cumulus and cirrus was known to many landscape painters in England and America. For the earth-bound John Ruskin, the ordinary cumulus, found in the central cloud region, was banal. He found real inspiration in the nimbus, the rain cloud of the lower cloud region. These are also the clouds that produce rainbows and the most magnificent sunsets, all of which we enjoy on the West Coast, a land made for painting skies. I share with Ruskin a love of nimbus.

In landscape, the sky, with its endlessly changing moods, is the source of all light. It would be difficult to find a landscape in which the sky did not play the most prominent role, from Constable's matter-of-fact naturalism to Turner's impressionistic rendering of atmospheric effects. Clouds in paintings are the provocative offspring of observation, aesthetics and science.

In Tumbo Channel, late in the day, when the sun was a white blaze, low and broad in the sky, all was simplified into light and shape. With the leaden-coloured east behind me, I stared into the light and painted the luminous void with a few reeling clouds.

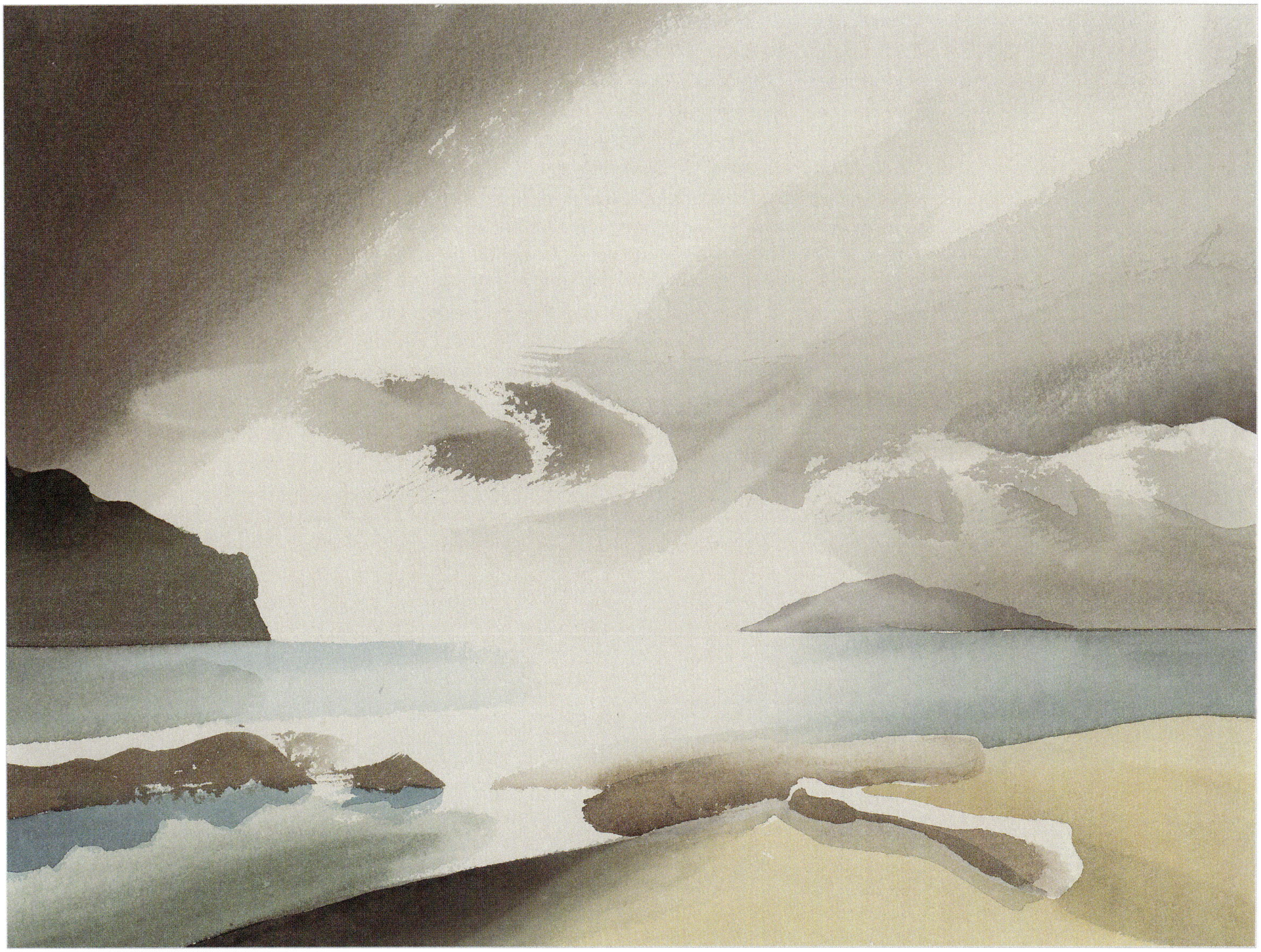

Tumbo Channel, Gulf Islands, 7 April 1991

POWDER MOUNTAIN

For years before I bought a ski-plane in Poland, I would overfly the glaciers of our coastal range from Vancouver to Alaska. I promised myself that one day I would have an airplane equipped to land on their virgin snows. When that day came and for the next three years, I painted almost exclusively on glaciers. I flew from glacier to glacier with my watercolours until one day, as recounted elsewhere in this book, an unexpected force of wind hurled my ski-plane into a deep ice crevasse.

Since I was pushing the envelope of freedom, it was probably only a matter of time. I had always felt very small high on these mountain slopes. I felt, as Rudolf Steiner put it, that I had to fight to "keep the great dark chords from sounding" with thoughts of unseen crevasses and impending avalanches. Nevertheless, I was drawn to these rarefied solitudes where the elemental landscape was an ideal subject for my brush.

I miss those days when I stepped out of my airplane at 8,000 feet onto virgin snow and into a deafening silence. I miss spreading my watercolours out on the tailplane in those cold, Spartan landscapes where a sudden storm could end my life.

I am shut out of the high mountains today, because my flying boat cannot land on glaciers. But the rest of the province is there for me: the lakes, the beaches, the islands, the many landing strips which are gateways to different landscapes.

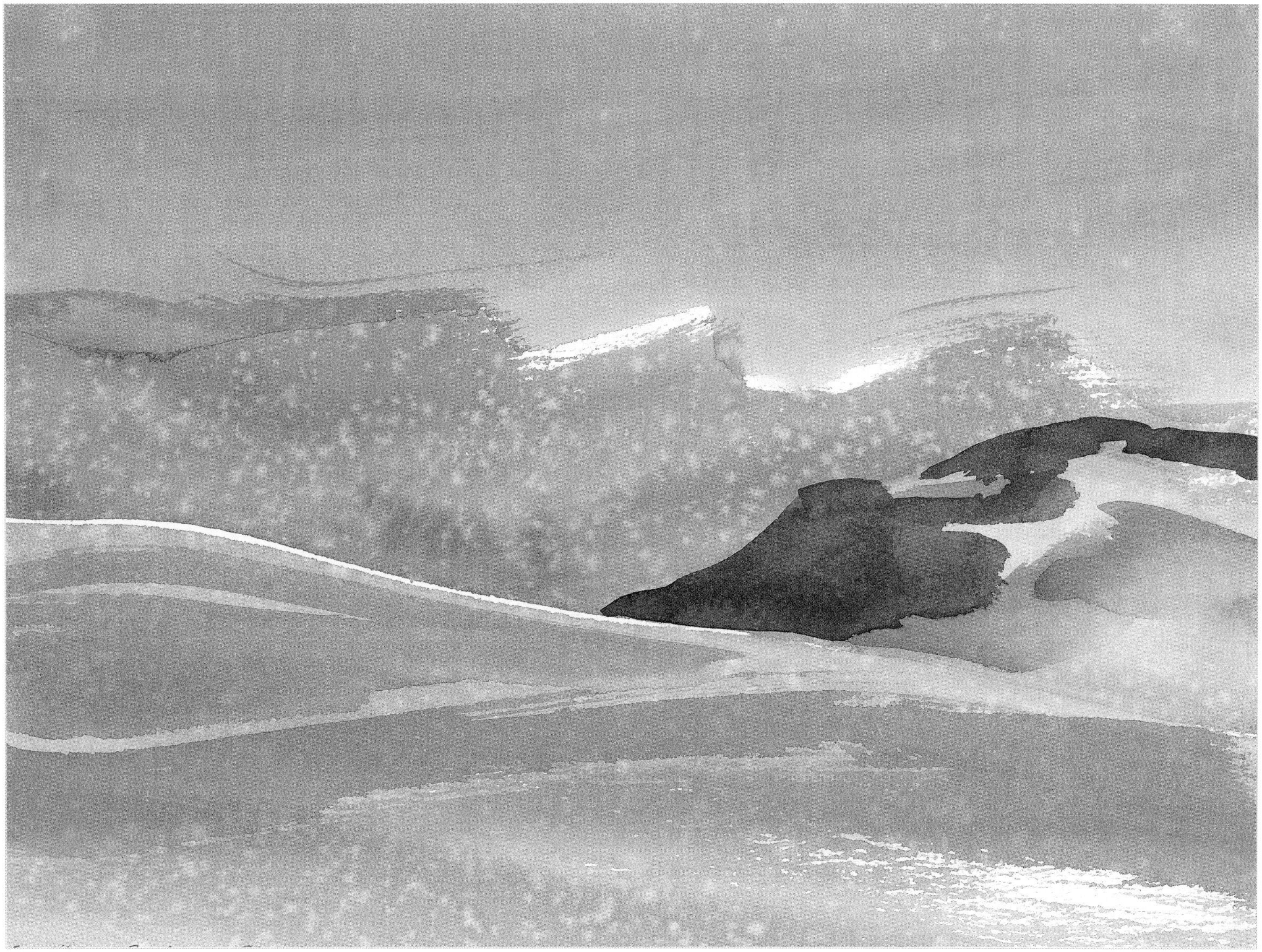

Snow Shower, Powder Mountain, September 5, 1982

CAPE FREEMAN MORESBY ISLAND QUEEN CHARLOTTE ISLANDS

I had often seen the clouds gathering off the coast over the Queen Charlottes, though the islands themselves were hidden in soft rains and mists. But I had never ventured across the ninety miles of open water until August of 1981, when I was invited to a painting trip around South Moresby as a guest of Bill Ellis aboard his charter boat, the *Singlejack*. I was to join fellow artists Joe Plaskett and Jim Willer.

For safety's sake I followed the coastal islands northwest to Terror Point on Banks Island, then swung west out over the open waters of Hecate Strait, heading for Sandspit. Terror Point and Hecate Strait – there can be a disturbing simplicity to the names left by mariners. Searching the horizon, I saw no sign of the Charlottes, only a dimpled blanket of soft, gray cloud.

Flying into a strong headwind, I felt suspended, motionless. Through holes in the clouds below I could glimpse the whitecaps of Hecate Strait, a sea that never gives up its dead. And then, after what felt like an eternity of standing still, I was looking down a deep, dark well into soft, black islands, floating in fathomless waters. These islands had existed in my imagination for as long as I could remember. Now I was seeing them for the first time, shrouded in mist and welling up from the green-black depths of sheltered bays and inlets.

Later, cruising on the *Singlejack* among the islands at the southern end of the archipelago, we anchored and set to work. I tried to paint my watercolours with all the capricious spontaneity that the weather exhibited, adding cloud shadows over soft, green hills as they appeared or grabbing a fresh sheet of white paper as the islands were gathered up in mists to dissolve and evaporate, then reappear, as if at the whim of a great magician. At times the scene would alter so quickly that I had to fix the light and shadow in my mind and not look back at the changing landscape, painting forever faster, running down to the galley to dry my watercolours over the oil stove so I could continue.

South Moresby is among those rare and sacred places on this earth where one can rediscover the primitive consciousness of being in this world. In the days that followed, I became a part of them and they became a part of me. I now hold them within me to carry always, just as I do the Isle of Man where I was born.

The Queen Charlottes are part of the geography of the Canadian imagination, like the Canadian Arctic. These last remaining islands of untouched wilderness are our greatest natural resource. They are sanctuaries, ours in trust only, to be always retained as they are, for future generations to explore with brush and pen.

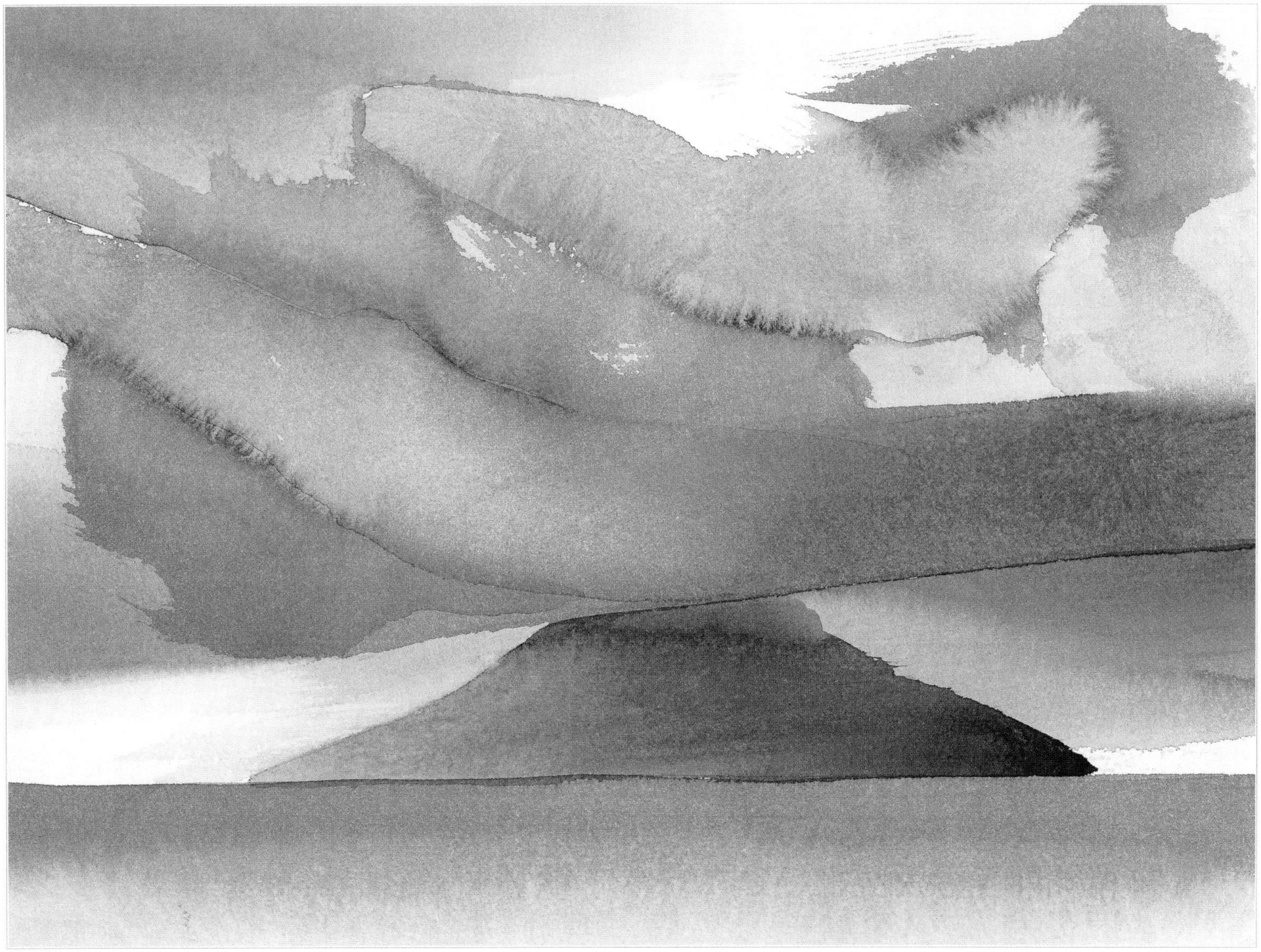

Clouds, Cape Freeman, Moresby Island, Queen Charlotte Islands, August 26, 1981

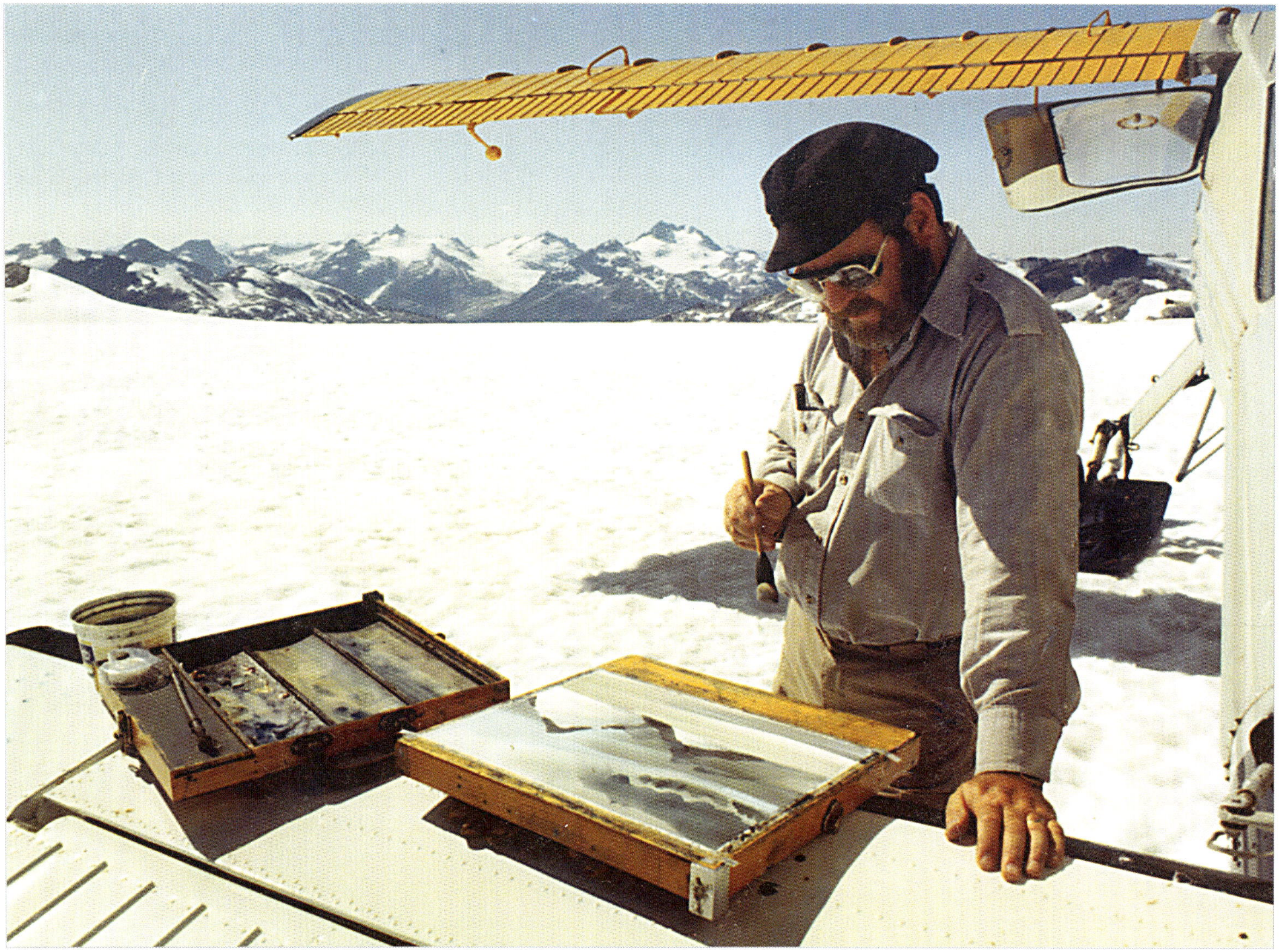

Toni Onley painting on Ubyssey Glacier in Garibaldi Park

NOTES ON MY WATERCOLOUR PALETTE, BRUSHES AND PAPER

If you whisper "watercolour" in the ear of someone at a party, images dance in the mind of eighteenth- and nineteenth-century ladies on the "grand tour," clutching little sketchbooks and a box of watercolours, doing, in the words of Dylan Thomas, "pale lady watercolours like a lettuce dying." Watercolour paintings are sometimes thought of as minor, mediocre achievements, hardly in the same league as oil paintings.

Watercolour is usually the first painting medium given to children. (A box of watercolours on my sixth birthday started me painting.) But it is also the medium of choice of some of England's greatest artists, such as Cozens, Girtin, Constable, Cotman and Turner, who produced some of the most profound works of art ever, in watercolour. The watercolour painter David Milne is generally regarded as one of Canada's greatest artists, and some of the finest achievements in American painting by such artists as Homer, Sargent, Marin, Feininger, Hopper, to name only a few, are in watercolour. Historically, Asian painting has been done almost exclusively in watercolour. If all the world's painting were reduced to only that produced in watercolour, we would still have some of the best works of our greatest artists.

Watercolour is the most portable means of painting ever devised. A stack of fifty watercolour papers is only an inch thick and the smallest watercolour box can go into a pocket, which is how Turner often carried his soft-covered watercolour palette. Dry watercolours he stuck to the leather folding cover of an old almanac that could be carried in his inside coat pocket.

Thirty years ago I designed for myself a painting box that could carry fifty sheets of paper, a complete palette of large No. 5 (14 ml) tubes of Winsor and Newton watercolours, a large Chinese goat hair brush and a collapsible Japanese water container. One half of the box contains mixing trays and a sliding lid compartment for tubes of paint. The other half contains my paper cut to 30 cm by 40 cm (11" x 15") and another long compartment for extra tubes of colour for longer trips. There is also room for the translucent Scotch tape I use to attach my paper to the box lid, which serves as a drawing board.

I travel with my watercolour box like a violinist with his violin case. The musician and the watercolour painter have in their hands two of the most direct means of expression ever devised, and either may give a virtuoso performance.

However, when you face a landscape with a loaded brush and a blank sheet of paper, the finale is not always a success. Attitude is everything. I tell my students, it's only a piece of paper and if you muck it up, it's not the end of the world; turn it over or grab a new sheet. The secret is to never make up your mind before starting what the painting will look like when finished – never draw before painting. Let the brush speak to you, regard every stroke and let the painting itself tell you when to stop. It is often what is not painted that counts in the end – the masses of dark that reveal the white, untouched paper. The Chinese artist Chang Yen-Yüan, c. 845 A.D., said:

> *He who deliberates and moves the brush intent upon making a picture, misses to a still greater extent the art of painting, while he who cogitates and moves the brush without such intentions, reaches the art of painting. His hands will not get stiff; his heart will not grow cold; without knowing how, he accomplishes it.*

The joy of painting landscape in watercolour comes from the speed of execution; the work is drying as you paint. In the shortest time it is possible, if you are completely focused, to have a painting which actually speaks to you. Landscape watercolour calls for a Zen-like oneness with Nature and an understanding of the essence of the paper and the watercolour interacting. The painter must also be sensitively aware of the part that temperature and humidity play. The rich simplicity of the British Columbia landscape is well suited to watercolour.

COLOURS

I have used Winsor and Newton watercolours all my life. Nothing short of perfection was good enough for the combined talents of the scientists William Winsor and the artist Henry Newton when they established their firm in 1832. They rapidly earned a reputation for quality which the firm enjoys to this day. I usually carry with me the 14 ml No. 5 tubes, their largest size; that way, I am less likely to run out of a colour on an extended painting trip, such as a summer in the Arctic, the Yukon or northern British Columbia.

French Ultramarine is an indispensable colour. It can be used with a variety of colours to produce rich grays. For instance, adding Sepia to French Ultramarine will produce a rich, velvety gray or, as I like to call it, a West Coast gray, while adding Light Red will produce a slightly more opaque, pearly gray, like the grays produced by adding Burnt Sienna or Burnt Umber.

Winsor Blue is W&N's replacement for Prussian Blue, which is fugitive. A deep, intense blue with a slight green tint, it is a powerful colour and one that I have always used. The admixture of Burnt Sienna will produce a brownish green or olive colour. Winsor Blue is too intense to be used in its pure state and is usually mixed.

Cobalt Blue is a gentle blue. It is a colour that I sometimes use in its pure state, a good sky colour. It too will produce beautiful grays, such as a clean, silvery gray, when mixed with Light Red or Cadmium Red.

Antwerp Blue is a colour I have used since 1976. That summer, when I was at Emma Lake in Saskatchewan, a student presented the colour to me saying, "Toni, I think this is 'your' colour," and I have used it ever since. Its slight greenish tint makes it not unlike Winsor Blue, but it is not as intense, so I often use it unmixed.

Winsor Green is a phthalocyanine green, the only green in my palette. It is more versatile than Viridian, which I used in my youth, and today it is an indispensable colour for me. In a pure state, it is very intense. The admixture of Brown Madder (Alizarin) will produce the dense greens of the West Coast rainforest. When mixed with Alizarin Crimson, it will produce a less intense gray-green, while a range of greens can be created by combining any of the yellows or browns with it.

Yellow Ochre is one of the oldest colours known to us. It will produce beautifully pale greens when mixed with the blues. With the admixture of Lamp Black, it will create the colour of wet sand. It is a more lively colour than Raw Sienna, but is not as transparent.

Raw Umber has a grayish tinge to it. With French Ultramarine, it will produce a beautiful gray; with Winsor Blue, a muddy green. When added to Winsor Green, a different scale of greens is created.

Burnt Umber will produce an intense bottle green when mixed with Winsor Green, while a pearly sky gray can be obtained with French Ultramarine.

Permanent Violet is a useful colour which I use in place of Cobalt Violet, an expensive colour. When mixed with Sepia, it produces a mysterious violet brown and when mixed with Raw Sienna, an equally strange colour. It is a colour that invites experiment.

Raw Sienna is similar to a dark ochre but far more transparent. Its admixture to any gray will warm the gray considerably. With the addition of Lamp Black, it makes a good sand colour. It will produce a range of greens when added to Antwerp Blue or Winsor Blue or Winsor Green.

Burnt Sienna is another good colour for producing greens and grays. Used with Winsor Blue and Winsor Green, it will produce an interesting scale of greens, while a deep, stormy gray is produced by mixing it with French Ultramarine.

Brown Madder is related to Alizarin Crimson and is beautifully transparent. With Winsor Green, it will produce the intense green of a West Coast forest. It can be used with Winsor Blue to obtain rich blue and violet tones. With Lamp Black, it makes a translucent brown.

Alizarin Crimson is strong but transparent and has the unusual characteristic of "separating" from other colours with which it is mixed, much like Cobalt Violet, as its crystals rise to the surface. It is useful for reducing the intensity of other colours, such as the greens and blues. When mixed with Winsor Blue, it creates beautiful grayish greens.

Light Red is an earth colour and is used almost exclusively for making grays, but it can also be mixed with Winsor Green to render it mossy – a gritty green, somewhat like a dry, olive green. When mixed with Ultramarine Blue or Cobalt Blue, it will produce a great range of warm to cool grays.

Cadmium Red is mixed with Cobalt Blue when a pure silver gray is required

Cadmium Yellow mixed with Antwerp Blue yields a very clear, light green.

Sepia is a colour that is very soluble and is almost like a warm black, useful in "knocking down" or muting the harsh intensity of some colours. It produces the richest of dark greens when mixed with Winsor Green or the stormiest of black grays when mixed with French Ultramarine. In the eighteenth and nineteenth centuries, it was used exclusively for wash drawings.

Lamp Black was a pigment that my first art teacher John Hobbs Nicholson did not allow his students to use because he believed that it demonstrated a lack of will and a lack of invention. Black was to be produced by mixing French Ultramarine with Burnt Sienna. But the black that is so produced is inadequate; it is really not black at all, but a rich dark gray. Lamp Black is the most transparent of the blacks; it is used to darken other colours, to give them a depth that is present when all light is absorbed. Used in a wash, it seems to crystallize, suspending tiny particles of pigment, imparting the wash with a special beauty. A distinctive range of greens is produced when it is mixed with Winsor Green. It generally changes or reduces the intensity of other colours, such as blues.

BRUSHES

The brush I use for my watercolours is a Chinese brush made of goat hair and is much larger, fatter and longer than an ordinary sable watercolour brush. When purchased, a goat hair brush (available in many sizes) is stiff, as the hairs are held together by a dry starch. Chinese or Japanese calligraphers usually soften the tip to the width required for their brush strokes. My brush is softened completely. When wet, it can be brought to a point with a flick of the wrist. It is capable of holding a great deal of water or pigment. If its water is removed, it will absorb water and pigment off the paper. It is durable and takes much rough treatment. The artist can twist it, turn it, even scrub the paper with it. Once an artist knows its ways, it is most responsive. Its versatility surpasses that of all other brushes.

The Chinese goat hair brush is entirely different from the traditional sable watercolour brushes I once painted with. Although I still use a sable No. 12 brush to paint postcard-size watercolours, I generally find sable to be too stiff for the kind of work I do. I prefer the soft and pliable Chinese brushes because they can produce surprising, spontaneous effects. With these big, floppy brushes, I can create a dialogue between myself and my work as it unfolds before me.

The Chinese writer on painting, Kuo Jo-hsü, wrote in Sung dynasty times:

> *The brush must be nimble, move swiftly in a continuous and connecting manner, so that the flow of life is not interrupted as the thoughts precede the brush. But the brush is also in the thoughts and when the picture is finished, all the thoughts are there and the image corresponds completely to the spirit. When the painter is inwardly serene, when his spirit is at ease and his thoughts calm, the mind is not exhausted and the brush not restrained.*

I also use a very large goat hair brush for Sumi ink drawings. For calligraphic elements in some of my collages, I use thinner, longer-haired Japanese calligraphy brushes. And to get a certain quality of line in some of my landscape paintings, I use brushes made entirely from a stick of bamboo. For these brushes, lengths of green bamboo are pounded into thin strands up to the first knot, then left to dry and mature. The result is a hard, stately bristle which produces a brittle line or broken shape when dragged on the paper. It is scratchy and very expressive – almost primitive in character. I have made my own bamboo brushes from stalks I found in my garden in Vancouver.

My goat hair brushes are special to me. When they wear out, they are not disposed of lightly. In an occasional private ritual, I will bring the old and new brushes to the landscape. I will work with one or both and, when I am finished painting, I will leave the old brush on the land, under a rock or in a log or tree, returning it to nature whence it came. This parallels an old Japanese custom (fude-zuku) of burying brushes with ceremony in a special "brush grave."

PAPER

In my watercolour painting, I am constantly experimenting with different papers. For many years, I painted on a French paper: a smooth *Velin Arches* rag paper. It was not heavily sized, as many English-made papers are, and had just the right absorbency for my needs.

Individual papers have varying degrees of absorbency: some papers absorb the paint so quickly as to allow no changes or corrections at all, while others give the painter a short time to make changes before the paint dries. Highly absorbent papers tend to produce the richest colours.

In the 1970s, beginning with my Arctic trips, I also used a new English paper called *T.H. Saunders*, which had more absorbency. It was not unlike oriental papers and, like them, quite unforgiving when it came to correcting errors. But the colour sank rapidly into this paper, thus retaining its rich intensity when dry.

Many of my watercolours have also been done on *David Cox Drawing*, an oatmeal-toned paper, favoured in the late nineteenth and early twentieth centuries, which is no longer manufactured. Thirty years ago, I was fortunate to find two quires (fifty imperial sheets) in a Victoria, B.C. art supply shop which the owner was happy to sell to me at a good discount. One of the best handmade paper mills in North America is Twinrocker, in Indiana. I sent them a sample of David Cox Drawing and asked them if they could make a paper like it. They made two papers for me of the weight I prefer, about 140 lb. One, called *Double X*, is an oatmeal tan colour; the other, *Ray's Gray*, is a warm, pale gray. Both these papers have all the qualities of my beloved David Cox Drawing.

Most of the works in this book were done on 140 lb. *Opus Watermedia* paper, a paper made for Opus Framers, my art supply source in Vancouver. I paint on the smooth side of this paper. It is a rag paper, not unlike a smooth Velin Arches but less expensive. Three paintings were done on other paper: *Tumbo Channel* on Double X and *Snow Shower, Powder Mountain* and *Clouds, Cape Freeman, Moresby Island* on T. H. Saunders.

It is important to discover which paper suits the needs of the individual artist. It is not possible to get good results in watercolour by using cheap paper or paper not designed to receive watercolour paint. Good rag paper is expensive; even so, I tell my students to buy a dozen sheets or more. If you buy only one sheet, you will feel that whatever you do has to be perfect. With that attitude, you are already programmed for failure and will not be in a fit state to follow the song of the brush.

ACKNOWLEDGEMENTS

I am profoundly grateful to my late friend George Woodcock for encouraging me to write about at least some of my travels and to my mechanic, Viggo Petersen, for keeping my planes flying for over thirty years.

ALSO BY TONI ONLEY:

A Silent Thunder, 1981
The Walls of India, George Woodcock and Toni Onley, 1985
Voyage en Artique, Toni Onley and Claude Péloquin, 1987
Onley's Arctic, 1989